Karlstadt's Battle with Luther

Karlstadt's Battle with Luther

Documents in a Liberal-Radical Debate

EDITED BY

RONALD J. SIDER

Wipf and Stock Publishers
150 West Broadway • Eugene OR 97401
2001

Karlstadt's Battle with Luther

Documents in a Liberal-Radical Debate

By Sider, Ronald J.

ISBN: 1-57910-779-6

Reprinted by *Wipf and Stock Publishers*
150 West Broadway • Eugene OR 97401

Previously published by Augsburg Fortress Press, 1978.

To all who yearn to be
both faithful and effective
in the struggle
to seek justice and correct oppression

Contents

Abbreviations

Abbreviations

ABK-B	Hermann Barge, *Andreas Bodenstein von Karlstadt* (2 vols.; Leipzig: Friedrich Brandstetter, 1905).
ABK-S	Ronald J. Sider, *Andreas Bodenstein von Karlstadt: The Development of His Thought 1517–1525* (Leiden; E. J. Brill, 1974).
Freys-Barge	H. Barge and E. Freys, "Verzeichnis der gedruckten Schriften des Andreas Bodenstein von Karlstadt," *Zentralblatt für Bibliothekswesen,* 21 (1904), 153–79, 209–43, 305–23.
Götze	Alfred Götze, *Frühneuhochdeutsches Glossar* (7th ed.; Berlin: Walter de Gruyter, 1967).
Hertzsch 1, 2	Erich Hertzsch, ed., *Karlstadts Schriften aus den Jahren 1523–1525* (2 vols.; Halle: Max Niemeyer, 1956–57).
LW	Martin Luther, *Luther's Works*, American edition, ed. Helmut T. Lehmann and Jaroslav J. Pelikan (55 vols.; Philadelphia: Fortress Press, 1955ff.).
St. L.	*D. Martin Luthers sämmtliche Schriften*, ed. J. G. Walch (23 vols.; St. Louis: Concordia Publishing House, 1880–1910).
WA	Martin Luther, *D. Martin Luthers Werke* (Weimar: Hermann Böhlau, 1833ff.).
WA, Br	*D. Martin Luthers Werke.* Briefwechsel (Weimar: Hermann Böhlau, 1930–48).
WB	Nikolaus Müller, *Die Wittenberger Bewegung 1521*

und 1522 (2d ed.; Leipzig: M. Heinsius Nachfolger, 1911).

WM James S. Preus, *Carlstadt's* Ordinaciones *and Luther's Liberty: A Study of the Wittenberg Movement, 1521–1522* (Cambridge: Harvard University Press, 1974).

Preface

The translations of all the Karlstadt material in this volume are my own. Ulrich Bubenheimer and Hans Kropatscheck graciously looked over parts of my translation, but they bear no responsibility for any remaining inadequacies. In the Karlstadt material, the scriptural quotations and paraphrases have been translated directly from Karlstadt's text; the page numbers in brackets refer to pages of the German text from which the translations were made; V refers to "verso."

Throughout the book, brackets are used for editorial comment; parentheses are part of the original document. An ellipsis signifies the omission of only a sentence or two. A full line of ellipsis points indicates the omission of a paragraph or more of the original document.

Because of the stringent limitations of space and because Luther's writings are readily accessible in the American edition of *Luther's Works,* only excerpts of the two Luther pieces are printed here. The Karlstadt items on the other hand are largely complete (except for the final selection from a particularly lengthy treatise). Footnotes frequently indicate what material has been omitted. Readers desiring a fuller historical orientation than that provided in the Introduction and at the beginning of each chapter may wish to turn first to a more extended description of the sixteenth century encounter contained in the interpretive essay at the end of the book (see the Conclusion).

For their indispensable assistance at the typewriter, I want to thank Brenda Hess, Debbie Reumann, and Donna Clark.

Introduction

When Martin Luther (1483–1546) tacked his Ninety-five Theses to the church door at Wittenberg on October 31, 1517, he triggered a chain of events which significantly shaped the course of Western history for the next four hundred years. A relatively obscure monk and theology professor until the posting of the famous theses, Luther became known almost overnight all over Western Europe. For three dramatic decades he occupied center stage in European religious and political life.

Luther, however, did not create the Reformation by himself. In recent decades Reformation scholars have paid increasing attention to the major "secondary" reformers who aided and abetted—and sometimes challenged and infuriated—Luther, Zwingli, and Calvin.[1] Karlstadt was one of the most important of these secondary reformers.

Andreas Bodenstein von Karlstadt (c. 1480–1541) was first a friend and ally, and then a bitter foe, of the more famous reformer of Wittenberg.[2] As a prominent professor of theology at Wittenberg, Karlstadt promoted Luther to the doctorate in 1512. Disagreement with Luther over whether the scholastic theologians understood Augustine[3] led to a new understanding of Augustine in early 1517. As a result, when Luther's Ninety-five Theses ignited controversy throughout Europe, Karlstadt was ready to do battle as an ardent polemicist for the new Wittenberg theology. It was

1. See, e.g., David C. Steinmetz, *Reformers in the Wings* (Philadelphia: Fortress, 1971).

2. For the subsequent biographical information, see *ABK-S*.

3. See Ernst Kähler, *Karlstadt und Augustin: Der Kommentar des Andreas Bodenstein von Karlstadt zu Augustins Schrift de Spiritu et Litera* (Halle: Max Niemeyer, 1952), pp. 3–10, esp. p. 4. Also, *WA*, Br 1, 65–66.

Karlstadt whom John Eck first challenged to the important debate at Leipzig in 1519. From 1518 through 1521 Karlstadt rushed into print a flood of books developing and defending the new Wittenberg theology. When the bull of excommunication was published in October 1520, Karlstadt's name along with Luther's appeared as a teacher of damnable heresy. Together they defied the pope.

Total harmony, however, did not always prevail between Wittenberg's two leading theologians. Luther's anger five years later over a private dispute apropos who should debate first at Leipzig in 1519[4] suggests that the two men never liked each other very well personally. In 1520 their first public disagreement surfaced. When Karlstadt began a series of lectures on James in 1520 Luther poked fun at the epistle because he disliked its emphasis on works. Luther's satirical opposition apparently decreased Karlstadt's audience and threatened their friendship.[5] In spite of this minor disagreement, however, the two men's theologies continued to converge in 1520–21.[6]

When Frederick the Wise "kidnapped" Luther and hid him in the safe seclusion of the Wartburg castle after the dramatic encounter with the emperor Charles V at Worms in April 1521, Karlstadt and the young humanist Melanchthon were the most influential leaders left at Wittenberg. As they moved from theological debate to practical implementation in the fall of 1521 and early 1522, however, occasional violence resulted, and Karlstadt was, to a very large degree, unjustly blamed for the disorder.[7] When Luther abruptly returned to assume leadership at Wittenberg in March 1522, he reversed most of the reforms Karlstadt had initiated. Karlstadt was disgraced and furious, and in 1523 moved to the important Saxon town of Orlamünde where he was able to introduce his more radical program of reform. In 1524 Karlstadt initiated the important sacramentarian controversy of the 1520s and, by attacking Luther's doctrine of the Real Presence, contributed to the division of Protestantism. Expelled from Saxony, Karlstadt spent his later years teaching at the University of Basel.

4. For what little is known of this, see below, p. 46, n. 25.

5. See Karlstadt's *De canonicis scripturis libellus*, reprinted in K. A. Credner, *Zur Geschichte des Canons* (Halle, 1847), pp. 371–72. In August 1519, Luther had questioned the book's apostolic authorship (*WA* 2, 425).

6. See *ABK-S*, pp. 45–70, 104–47.

7. See the note on p. 16 and p. 25, n. 7.

Most scholars have explained the bitter quarrel between Luther and Karlstadt in terms of major theological differences.[8] But careful analysis of Karlstadt's theology in 1521 reveals few significant theological disagreements.[9] Like Luther, Karlstadt strongly affirmed *sola scriptura,* the necessity of literal exegesis, and the mediation of grace via the external word. As the sermon translated below in chapter 1 clearly shows, Karlstadt's primary understanding of *justitia* in 1520 and 1521 was of that imputed righteousness which is reckoned to the believer who trusts in Christ's promise. Although Karlstadt employed the words "justification" and "gospel" less than Luther, he certainly believed deeply in forensic justification. By 1521 Karlstadt had rejected his earlier Augustinian notion of eternal life as the reward of divinely bestowed good deeds and adopted Luther's view that, since even the best deeds are tainted with sin, faith alone must be the sole ground of eternal salvation. Karlstadt also adopted Luther's doctrine of the priesthood of all believers, and his eucharistic writings are largely a repetition of Luther's ideas.

To be sure, there were differences. Karlstadt rejected oral confession.[10] He condemned as sinful the communicant who followed medieval tradition and took only the bread.[11] Most important, he believed that the Old Testament was normative for Christians in a way that Luther feared would undermine Christian freedom.[12] But the disagreements were relatively few and must not obscure the fact that Luther and Karlstadt were in fundamental theological agreement up to the time Luther returned to Wittenberg in March 1522 to squelch Karlstadt's reforms.

Why then the violent confrontation?

8. See, for instance, Friedel Kriechbaum, *Grundzüge der Theologie Karlstadts* (Hamburg—Bergstedt: Herbert Reich Evangelischer Verlag, 1967); Walther Köhler in *Göttingische gelehrte Anzeigen,* 174 (1912), 505–50; C. F. Jäger, *Andreas Bodenstein von Carlstadt* (Stuttgart, 1856); Ernst Wolf, "Gesetz und Evangelium in Luthers Auseinandersetzung mit den Schwärmern," *Evangelische Theologie,* 5 (1938), 96–109.

9. See *ABK-S,* pp. 104–47.

10. See below, pp. 12–14.

11. See Karlstadt's Theses (Nos. 9–10) of July 17, 1521, quoted in *ABK-S,* p. 144, n. 188. But see *WM,* p. 21 for a discussion of the reason for this prohibition. Luther rejects Karlstadt's view in *LW* 48, 279–81.

12. See, e.g., *Von abtuhung der Bylder* (1522), reprinted in Hans Lietzmann, ed., *Andreas Karlstadt: Von Abtuhung der Bilder* (Bonn, 1911), p. 21; for additional examples see *ABK-S,* pp. 108–12. Luther's concern for freedom is evident below, pp. 25–30, 97, 108–10.

The thesis of both my earlier study of Karlstadt[13] and also this book is that to a far greater extent than has been realized Luther and Karlstadt fell out because of disagreement over strategy, tactics, and timing. James S. Preus has supported this view in his recent study of the Wittenberg Movement where he argues that

> the fundamental issues in 1521–22 were issues of religious *policy,* and that important aspects of the doctrinal profiles by which Lutheran and "radical" are identified are as much a *function* of the religio-political struggle and the result of reflection upon the outcome of that crisis, as they are a *cause* of the breakup of the movement. To be sure, the theologies of Karlstadt and Luther were by no means identical in 1521–22, but neither were theological differences the decisive reason for their separation.[14]

One cannot satisfactorily explain the break between Luther and Karlstadt primarily in terms of theological differences. In 1522 their disagreement was far more over strategy than over theology, and the two must not be confused.

As the subtitle of this book suggests, the modern debate over strategy between liberals and radicals helps illuminate Luther's and Karlstadt's disagreement. A final interpretative chapter develops this thesis at some length.[15]

13. *ABK-S,* pp. 104–201.

14. *WM,* p. 2 (Preus's italics). In a somewhat similar way Ulrich Bubenheimer speaks of "a problem less of the content of reform than of strategies of reform." "Scandalum et ius divinum: Theologische und rechtstheologische Probleme der ersten reformatorischen Innovationen in Wittenberg 1521/22," *Zeitschrift der Savigny-Stiftung für Rechtsgeschichte* (1973), p. 287. Bubenheimer, however, also tends to emphasize Karlstadt's "legalism" and "biblicism."

15. See below, Conclusion. For the definitions of "liberal" and "radical" used throughout, see n. 9 of the Conclusion, below, pp. 140–41.

1
Karlstadt as Reformer: The Sermon for the First Evangelical Eucharist

Immediately after Luther's daring defiance of the emperor at Worms in April 1521, Frederick the Wise of Saxony hid Luther in the secluded Wartburg castle for a year. During Luther's year-long absence from Wittenberg Karlstadt and other associates of Luther proceeded to implement some of the changes required by the new theology.

On Christmas day, 1521, Karlstadt celebrated the first public evangelical Eucharist of the Reformation. For some time, Luther and Karlstadt had been writing vigorous polemics against the medieval view of the mass.* During the fall of 1521 small groups had met privately to receive both kinds. But the public services remained the same. Karlstadt's bold step—taken in defiance of the elector's prohibition against innovations—changed the situation dramatically.

Advance notice of the historic service and drunken rioting the previous night guaranteed a huge crowd. Dressed in a simple, secular gown, Karlstadt read a simplified Latin mass, omitting all references to sacrifice. For the first time in the Reformation the words of institution were spoken in German in a public service. Karlstadt declined to elevate the host. The tension reached its peak when, instead of placing the bread in each communicant's mouth, Karlstadt allowed ordinary lay persons to take the bread and the cup in their own trembling hands. This innovation so terrified one

* For Karlstadt's views see *Von den Empfahern, zeichen, und zusag des heyligenn Sacraments fleysch und bluts Christi*, June 24, 1521 (Freys-Barge, No. 54); *Von anbettung . . .*, November 1, 1521 (Freys-Barge, No. 68); *Von beiden gestaldten der heylige Messze*, November 30, 1521 (Freys-Barge, No. 71). Only the first of these is available in a modern reprint: *St. L.* 20, 2288–2307. For Luther's views see *The Babylonian Captivity of the Church* (1520), *LW* 36, 18–57; *The Blessed Sacrament* (December 1519), *LW* 35, 79–111. For a discussion of Karlstadt's dependence on Luther, see *ABK-S*, pp. 140–44.

frightened layman that he dropped his wafer and was too terror-stricken to pick it up.

The simple but powerful sermon Karlstadt preached on this historic occasion shows how similar his and Luther's theology were at this time.* Although the phrase is not used, the sermon contains a clear, forceful declaration of justification by faith alone. Other important Lutheran themes, such as faith in the promise of the words of institution and the external word as a means of grace, are also central to the sermon.

To be sure, Luther did not like the total rejection of oral confession (see pp. 33–35 below). Because of Karlstadt's sermon oral confession promptly decreased significantly at Wittenberg, and not even Luther's vigorous encouragement of the traditional practice after his return in 1522 was able to reinstate it quickly.

For more on the historical background, see below, pp. 147–49; *WM*, pp. 140–60; Wilhelm H. Neuser, *Die Abendmahlslehre Melanchthons in ihrer geschichtlichen Entwicklung (1519–1530)* (Neukirchen-Vluyn: Neukirchener Verlag, 1968), pp. 114–213; E. Fischer, *Zur Geschichte der evangelischen Beichte* (2 vols.; Leipzig, 1902–1903); *ABK*-S, pp. 140–60.

The following selections from this sermon are translated from a 1522 edition (Freys-Barge, No. 78) in the Yale University library.

* For a discussion of the extent and importance of theological disagreement at this time, see above, pp. 3–4. Even Luther acknowledged considerable theological agreement in his sermon of March 9, 1522 (see below, p. 17).

A Sermon of
Andreas Bodenstein von Karlstadt
at Wittenberg
Concerning the Reception of the Holy Sacrament
Wittenberg
[December 25, 1521]

To [AV] the little Christian congregation at Wittenberg.

. . . .

I. He who wants to know and learn what makes him unworthy of this blessed sacrament must pay attention to the narratives, history, and Scripture of the old law and diligently consider what made the Jews unworthy of divine promises and then compare the New Testament with the Old just as one compares the sun with the stars of heaven. Then he would undoubtedly notice and perceive what makes him unable to appropriate this sacrament. For nowhere can we learn of such unfitness except in the divine law.[1] As Paul says: "I would not have known of sin except for the law" (Rom. 3 [7:7]). You should be satisfied, certain, and assured that it is mere lies and invention when one tells you that this or that makes you incapable or unworthy of divine grace but cannot show you any Scripture.[2]

. . . .

VI. If [Aiv] one does not believe, to hear the word of the gospel or understand gracious and favorable tidings is certainly totally useless and of no help to anyone (Heb. 4 [:2]). Nor can

1. For the view that Karlstadt's legal training (he had a doctorate in canon and civil law as well as a doctorate in theology) led him to regard Scripture as divine law, see Ulrich Bubenheimer, *Consonantia theologiae et iurisprudentiae: Andreas Bodenstein von Karlstadt als Theologe und Jurist zwischen Scholastik und Reformation* (Tübingen: Mohr, 1977). Interesting in light of Karlstadt's and Luther's bitter disagreement over the value of the Mosaic law (see below, p. 102, n. 10) is Karlstadt's clear affirmation here of the superior authority of the New Testament.

2. In the four pages omitted, Karlstadt adduces Old Testament texts to prove that one dare not teach anything without scriptural authority, and that unbelief is the only thing that makes one unfit to receive the sacrament ("all unholiness, all unfitness arises out of unbelief" [Aiii]).

one enter into any peace and rest. As it stands written: I have sworn that if one will enter my rest [he must not harden his heart (cf. Heb. 3:7–15)]. Therefore when one hears God's Word, he should not harden his heart—that is, he should not be unbelieving. For unbelief causes unfitness, unworthiness and a hard heart and obtains God's anger and fury.

VII. Therefore no one should consider how he can make himself worthy of and receptive to this sacrament by prayer, fasting, confession, penance, and the like. For even if you had all of these things and had the repentance and good efforts of the whole world but lacked faith, you would be unworthy of this sacrament and not at all fit for it.

VIII. Nor may you fear sin, for Christ came to redeem and purify his people from their sin (Matt. 1 [:21]). Nor did Christ call only righteous persons, but rather only sinners (Matt. 9 [:13]). Likewise Christ has instituted the sacrament only for sinners. Therefore sins should inflame and drive you to run to this sacrament.

IX. Even though you had not gone to confession, you should still go joyfully in good confidence, hope, and faith and receive this sacrament. For it must always be true that faith alone makes us holy and righteous. This saying is certainly true: "Your faith has saved you" [Matt. 9:22]. Similarly: "All things are possible to him who believes" (Mark 9 [:23]).

X. He who has little faith receives little. He who has a strong and abundant faith obtains much. As Christ says: Be it done to you as you believe and as you desire (Matt. 8 [:13]; 15 [:28]).

XI. [AivV] You should not be afraid because of sin. For Moses says: You shall not fear them, for the Egyptians whom you now see you will see no more. You shall stand still and be quiet for it is God who works and fights for you (Exod. 14 [13–14]). When you receive this sacrament in true faith, you will see and fear the sin no more. For even though your conscience afflicts and accuses you, God is greater and more than your heart and he knows all things (I John 3 [:19–20]).

XII. Stand freely and boldly in your faith. Fear no deed or misdeed. God gives to all who call on him in faith, and reproaches no one for his wickedness (Jas. 1 [:5]). You dare not think: I have often angered God. Or: I have revolted against him sometimes; therefore he will say to me (as angry men sometimes speak to those who have moved them to anger): Should I help you? Should I be gracious to you? You have done this and this! No! God is gracious, kind, merciful, forbearing, and forgives evils (Jon. 4 [:2]). He remembers them no more (Isa. 43 [:25]) and does not reproach any believer with his guilt and villainy.

XIII. Only take care that you do not go in unbelief when you want to receive the sacrament. In that case God will say to you: Because you have not believed, you are unworthy of my consolation and you will not be able to see fruit and growth. Notice how Christ speaks to him who had not put on a wedding garment: Throw him into outer darkness [Matt. 22:13]. In this sacrament, you can do God no greater harm, you can insult and belittle him no more severely, than when you do not believe him. (That is shown above in articles II, III, IV, and V.)

XIV. Christ speaks conclusively: "He who believes in the Son of God is not condemned, but he who does not believe is already condemned because he has not believed in the name of the only-begotten Son of Christ" (John 3 [:18]). This faith grasps the word of Christ so that the man who believes in Christ comprehends the words and promises of Christ. Therefore [B] he says: "He who hears my word and believes in him who has sent me has eternal life and does not come into condemnation" (John 5 [:24]). Therefore he says: "He who keeps my word will never see death" (John 8 [:51]).

XV. Consequently fitness and worthiness depend on faith alone. To those who want to receive the sacrament, therefore, I can say nothing other than what Moses said: Fear not. Stand and you will see a great miraculous work of God (Exod. 14 [:13–14]; II Chron. 20 [:15]). Just stand in good confidence and you will become certain and will receive divine help.

XVI. Now someone may say: What should I believe in this sacrament? And on what should I stand? Here is the answer: You should believe the words of Christ, that is, the two gospels which Christ spoke to his dinner companions: "My body is given for you" and "My blood is shed for you for the forgiveness of sins." Those are the two promises which you should receive in your heart and which you must believe. For the mouth of the Lord has spoken them. If you do not believe them, you must die and you are spiritually dead before you eat the Lord's bread and wine—just as Aaron died because he did not believe the divine mouth (Num. 20 [:10ff., 24–26]). He who does not grasp these words in faith is entirely unworthy of this sacrament and cuts off Christ's honor. He injures and mocks him when he sits at his table. And he remembers the Lord as the Jews and Judas Iscariot remembered him, not as the disciples did.

XVII. Therefore you should pay attention to the way Christ speaks to you and what he says to you. Briefly, this pledge, my body is broken or given for you, promises a harmless death and a joyful resurrection to all men. For [BV] Christ died for us in order to destroy death. As it stands written: O death, I will be your death; I will bite and beat you to death (Hos. 13 [:14]).[3] Christ makes us certain that no death will lead us to damnation if we can believe that he destroyed our death. Thus death becomes a door and way to a better life and leads us not to hell or damnation but rather to life. For the one who now knows that, death, which previously was bitter and dreadful to him, becomes sweet and joyous, acceptable and pleasing. You receive this fruit from this promise, "My body is given for you." You also obtain certain hope of a joyful resurrection, for Christ says that his body is given for us. Christ kills our death with his death and brings us resurrection with his resurrection just as we are buried with Christ and participate in his death. Thus we are resurrected with him in certain hope and will also certainly arise. Christ has indicated that to us by saying: He who believes in me has eternal life and I will resurrect him at the last day. Likewise: He who eats my flesh and drinks my blood has eternal life (John 6 [:47, 54]). In this promise of Christ, we should obtain this and other blessed fruits such as the fulfillment of the law and the daily bearing of the cross of Christ—in short, all kinds of blessings which I cannot relate now.

XVIII. The sign of the bread produces nothing other than certainty and assurance of the aforesaid promise so that man should be certain in the bread and assured that God will graciously give him all that he has promised. You should think thus: Now I am certain and assured that Christ has said to me, "My body is given for you." And I am certain that death does not injure me but rather leads to a better and desired life. Likewise, I am so certain of and

3. Cf. the Vulgate: *"Ero mors tua o mors, morsus tuus ero inferne"* ["O death, I will be thy death; O hell, I will be thy bite"—Douay].

eager for the future life that because of eagerness I do not pay attention to death.

I am just like one who sees a great treasure through a hard rock and who because of the great joy does not feel the work and labor by which he splits the rock. I know that I will come to eternal life through death. Why then should I fear the bitterness of death? Why should I not struggle with it cheerfully? Why should I not taste it gladly?

XIX. The bread which you take also makes you certain that through Christ you can escape the anger and curse of the law, since Christ became a curse for all believers (Gal. 3 [:13]). You must think and say: I know that I am blessed in Christ and that the law can destroy me no more. For Christ makes me share in all his righteousness and fulfillment of the law.

XX. Thus I should also be certain that the injury of the cross will not harm me. For Christ stands before me and carries precisely that cross which he has given and laid upon me. In short, I must be assured that no devil, no hell, and no evil will harm me.

XXI. If it should occur to you that God punishes in righteousness even to the fourth generation, you should also reflect on the fact that God desires the life of man much more than his death. Take to heart the fact that Jonah feared God's mercy so much that he did not want to preach destruction to the city of Nineveh. He said: I know that you are a gracious, merciful, and forbearing God and you forgive evils. Therefore I fled and did not want to proclaim your threat. (Jon. 4 [:2ff.]).

XXII. The gospel (to which the drinking vessel or cup belongs) brings forgiveness of sins if you believe. For Christ says: My blood is shed for you for the forgiveness of sins. This saying purifies everyone who believes it, for faith makes God's Word useful only to those who receive the divine promise in faith (Heb. 4 [:2]). When you receive God's comforting promise [BiiV] in faith, you become pure and clean. Christ attests this when he says: "You are now pure because of the word which I have spoken to you" (John 15 [:3]). God's Word purifies and sanctifies all who receive it in faith. Therefore Christ says: O Father, make them holy through your truth [John 17:17]. See how Christ implores and begs his Father to make his disciples truly holy through his truth. Christ answers the heart which might ask, "What is the truth?" by saying:

Your speech or word is the truth which makes holy [John 17:17]. Now hear what Christ says next: "I make myself holy for them so that they are also sanctified through the truth" [John 17:19]. Notice here the boundless joy which Christ proclaims to his disciples. What could a disciple of Christ hear that would be more comforting than Christ's saying, "I make myself holy for the sake of my disciples." For with these words he says here secretly what he says openly in John 3 [:16–17]) and elsewhere: Each person who believes in me is saved. It is as if he wanted to say: You do not need any work or labor; nothing on earth is necessary for you except for you to look at me and believe that I am sent by my Father to save this world. See how Christ makes you share in his salvation if you believe. See how he sanctifies and purifies you through his promise. See yet further that Christ stands before you and frees you of all your work and takes all doubt from you so that you shall indeed know with certainty that he saves you through his Word. Now if God makes holy, he must certainly forgive sin. For it is written: Blessed are those whose sins are forgiven [Rom. 4:7]. He who now believes the divine truth and the gracious proclamation is holy. And it is impossible for Christ not to say to him: Arise, your faith has saved you. Arise, your sins are forgiven. But he who does not believe the Word [Biii] insults God, makes him unholy, mocks his Word, and is the swine who tramples the pearl under foot [Matt. 7:6] and the dog who barks against the divine Word and falls on the messengers with his teeth.

Here now,[4] you tell me this! If you say that I should or may drink the cup and its promise without going to confession, then I go to this sacrament wantonly as a sow.

I answer. Slowly, dear fellow! I ask you whether Christ speaks truly: Take it and drink. The drinking vessel is the new testament in my blood which is shed for you and for many for the forgiveness of sins. Likewise, I ask whether Christ speaks correctly: Make them holy through your word. If you believe that Christ has spoken this word correctly and truly, then you must certainly believe that he forgives sins if you grasp his word which he has given to the cup. Further, if you obtain forgiveness of sins beforehand in confession, what then do you want to do with the

4. Karlstadt states the argument of someone who might object to his sermon.

sacrament? Furthermore, if you want to have forgiveness of sins before you partake of the sacrament and then afterward receive the sacrament, then indeed you must have no faith in the words of Christ. It would be more useful for you to drink a swine's drink than to drink the Lord's cup. Or it would be more useful for you to eat donkey's manure than to eat the bread of Christ. Furthermore, when one does not believe the words of Christ, he is like the swine who tramples the little jewel in the filth or manure.

In addition, even if forgiveness of secret sins were obtained in oral confession (which I do not believe), you must certainly carry with you sins which the sacrament can remove. For the promise points to forgiveness of sins which this word cannot forgive if sins are not present. Furthermore, these words, "All that you bind shall be bound; all [BiiiV] that you loose shall be loosed" [Matt. 18:18], pertain to public sins. And although they include other sins, you cannot submit any more certain words of absolution than the aforesaid words about the cup. Nor can you point out any more beloved and precious words than the words of the cup. That is the reason Christ left them behind as his testament and commended them to us as his last will and related them to us before his bitter passion. You must pay very little attention or not even believe this passage if you dare not or will not seek forgiveness of sins in the gospel of the cup.

Briefly I want to advise that anyone who cannot believe that he can or will obtain forgiveness of sins through the sacrament of the cup should eagerly flee from this sacrament. For God speaks thus to Moses: Because Aaron has not believed my mouth, he will not enter the land which I have given to the children of Israel (Num. 20 [:12]). God thereby teaches us that one becomes unworthy of his promise at the moment and instant that he begins to doubt the divine promise. God wants to say the same [to us]: Because you do not believe what I speak and say to you, you shall therefore be deprived of my consolation. Indeed you must also be punished just as Aaron had to die.

It is certainly a wretched and horrible thing when I believe a priest when he absolves me, and cannot believe him when he speaks the word of Christ in the fashion, form, and way that Christ spoke it for the forgiveness of sins. It is nothing other than the devil's trick and the Antichrist's hovel when the word of the cup does not carry as much weight with one as the invented form of a miserable priest—especially since they [the papacy] ignore the only form of their authority from Christ which reads as follows: What you bind is bound; what you loose is loosed. That is a form and word of authority by which they may and can absolve and bind us laymen.[5] Gladly, however, would I like to see and hear them show me a [biblical] form and word for their absolution.

I [Biv] know well what form and word Paul observed when he threw out and separated the public sinner whom he gave to the devil for the destruction of his flesh (I Cor. 5 [:5]). Paul also took his form and word from Christ—that is, what we have written (Matt. 18 [:18]). Therefore it follows that no priest can bind without[6] a Christian congregation [*hauffen*]. For Paul says (I Cor. 5 [:4]): *Congregatis vobis et spiritu meo* [when you are gathered together and my spirit is present]. And Christ says (Matt. 15 [:17]): *Dic ecclesiae. Si non audierit ecclesiam,* etc. [Tell the church. If he will not hear the church, etc.] All that you will bind or loose is bound or loosed (Matt. 18 [:18]). Also, Christ gave Peter the keys when he answered for the whole group (Matt. 15 [16:16–19]).

XXIII. Now even if I granted that private confession were godly and good, you must also still admit to me that the word of the cup also forgives sins and that one obtains forgiveness of sins in the cup no less than in confession. As long then as the people turn their eyes on confession in such a way that they as little trust this word of the cup as they greatly trust confession, and cling to confession as much as they are strangers to the sacrament, I will consider that they do their confession because they do not seek forgiveness of sins in the reception of the sacrament. That is dangerous and harmful. . . .

I should stop. But it is necessary for me to point out further that God's Word received in faith purifies us. Christ speaks thus: You are pure because of the word which I have spoken to you (John 15 [:3]). The Word of God is pure. Therefore it must purify when it is grasped. Yes, the Word of God gives birth and makes new. He has given birth to us in the Word of his truth so that

5. This is a striking example of Karlstadt's identification with the laity and the common people.

6. *An* is the equivalent of *ohne*. See Götze.

[BivV] we would be the beginning of his spiritual creatures (Jas. 1 [:18]). See then how God gives birth to us in his Word and makes us a spiritual creature. I Pet. 1 [:23]) also says that: We have been born of an imperishable seed, through the Word of the living God.

. . . .

Peace be with you. Amen.

2
Radicalism Denounced: Luther's Eight Sermons at Wittenberg, 1522

Changes occurred quickly in Wittenberg in January of 1522. About January 24, the city council issued a decree authorizing the removal of images and regulating the eucharistic services along the lines of Karlstadt's celebration on Christmas day. The words of institution were to be spoken in German and the communicants were to take the bread and cup in their own hands. Private masses were abolished. In spite of Karlstadt's and the other leaders' opposition to disorders,* incidental rioting and vandalism against images occurred occasionally in December and January. This disorder plus the imperial government's mandate of January 20, 1522, which forbid all changes and ordered an official visitation of electoral Saxony by Catholic bishops, prompted the elector to end innovation in Wittenberg. In negotiations during February Karlstadt, Melanchthon, and the other leaders agreed to restore some of the old practices.

Then on March 6 Luther ended his year-long absence and returned to Wittenberg to take charge of his reformation which he feared had fallen into irresponsible hands. After private conversations for three days, Luther preached eight powerful sermons from March 9–16. He denounced the way the changes had been made, stressed the importance of Christian liberty, and outlined his views on the mass, images, fasting, partaking of both kinds, and oral confession. Immediately successful in reasserting his leadership, Luther restored virtually all the medieval practices abolished during the Wittenberg Movement. Karlstadt fell into disgrace.

For further discussion of the historical background see, in addition to the standard Luther biographies and histories of the Reformation: below, pp. 147–50, *WM*, pp. 60–88; Mark U. Edwards, *Luther and the False Brethren* (Stanford: Stanford University Press, 1975), pp. 6–33. The following selections from the Eight Sermons are from the translation by A. Steimle, revised by John W. Doberstein, in the American edition of *Luther's Works* 51, 70ff.

* On Karlstadt's opposition to disorder, see the documents in *WB*, No. 18, p. 48; No. 83, p. 181; No. 93, p. 195; and the analysis in *ABK-S*, pp. 168–69.

Eight Sermons by Dr. M. Luther, Preached by Him at Wittenberg in Lent Dealing Briefly with the Masses, Images, Both Kinds in the Sacrament, Eating [of Meats], and Private Confession, etc.

The First Sermon, March 9, 1522, Invocavit Sunday

The summons of death comes to us all, and no one can die for another. Everyone must fight his own battle with death by himself, alone. We can shout into another's ears, but everyone must himself be prepared for the time of death, for I will not be with you then, nor you with me. Therefore every one must himself know and be armed with the chief things which concern a Christian. And these are what you, my beloved, have heard from me many days ago.

In the first place, we must know that we are the children of wrath, and all our works, intentions, and thoughts are nothing at all. Here we need a clear, strong text to bear out this point. Such is the saying of St. Paul in Eph. 2 [:3]. Note this well; and though there are many such in the Bible, I do not wish to overwhelm you with many texts. "We are all the children of wrath." And please do not undertake to say: I have built an altar, given a foundation for masses, etc.

Secondly, that God has sent us his only-begotten Son that we may believe in him and that whoever trusts in him shall be free from sin and a child of God, as John declares in his first chapter, "To all who believed in his name, he gave power to become children of God" [John 1:12]. Here we should all be well versed in the Bible and ready to confront the devil with many passages. With respect to these two points I do not feel that there has been anything wrong or lacking. They have been rightly preached to you, and I should be sorry if it were otherwise. Indeed, I am well aware and I dare say that you are more learned than I, and that there are not only one, two, three, or four, but perhaps ten or more, who have this knowledge and enlightenment.

Thirdly, we must also have love and through love we must do to one another as God has done to us through faith. For without love faith is nothing, as St. Paul says (I Cor. 2 [13:1]): If I had the tongues of angels and could speak of the highest things in faith, and have not love, I am nothing. And here, dear friends, have you not grievously failed? I see no signs of love among you, and I observe very well that you have not been grateful to God for his rich gifts and treasures.

Here let us beware lest Wittenberg become Capernaum [cf. Matt. 11:23]. I notice that you have a great deal to say of the doctrine of faith and love which is preached to you, and this is no wonder; an ass can almost intone the lessons, and why should you not be able to repeat the doctrines and formulas? Dear friends, the kingdom of God—and we are that kingdom—does not consist in talk or words [I Cor. 4:20], but in activity, in deeds, in works and exercises. God does not want hearers and repeaters of words [Jas. 1:22], but followers and doers, and this occurs in faith through love. For a faith without love is not enough—rather it is not faith at all, but a counterfeit of faith, just as a face seen in a mirror is not a real face, but merely the reflection of a face [I Cor. 13:12].

Fourthly, we also need patience. For whoever has faith, trusts in God, and shows love to his neighbor, practicing it day by day, must needs suffer persecution. For the devil never sleeps, but constantly gives him plenty of trouble. But patience works and produces hope [Rom. 5:4], which freely yields itself to God and vanishes away in him. Thus faith, by much affliction and persecution, ever increases, and is strengthened day by day. A heart thus blessed with virtues can never rest or restrain itself, but rather pours itself out again for the benefit and service of the brethren, just as God has done to it.

And here, dear friends, one must not insist upon his rights, but must see what may be useful and helpful to his brother, as Paul says, *Omnia mihi licent, sed non omnia expediunt,* "'All things are lawful for me,' but not all things are helpful" [I Cor. 6:12]. For we are not all equally strong in faith, some of you have a stronger faith than I. Therefore we must not look upon ourselves, or our strength, or our prestige, but upon our neighbor, for God has said through Moses: I have borne and reared you, as a mother does her child [Deut. 1:31]. What does a mother do to her child? First she gives it milk, then gruel, then eggs and soft food, whereas if she turned about and gave it solid food, the child would never thrive [cf. I Cor. 3:2; Heb. 5:12-13]. So we should also deal with our brother, have patience with him for a time, have patience with his weakness and help him bear it; we should also give him milk-food, too [I Pet. 2:2; cf. Rom. 14:1-3], as was done with us, until he, too, grows strong, and thus we do not travel heavenward alone, but bring our brethren, who are not now our friends, with us. If all mothers were to abandon their children, where would we have been? Dear brother, if you have suckled long enough, do not at once cut off the breast, but let your brother be suckled as you were suckled. I would not have gone so far as you have done,[1] if I had been here. The cause is good, but there has been too much haste. For there are still brothers and sisters on the other side who belong to us and must still be won.

Let me illustrate. The sun has two properties, light and heat. No king has power enough to bend or guide the light of the sun; it remains fixed in its place. But the heat may be turned and guided, and yet is ever about the sun. Thus faith must always remain pure and immovable in our hearts, never wavering; but love bends and turns so that our neighbor may grasp and follow it. There are some who can run, others must walk, still others can hardly creep [cf. I Cor. 8:7-13]. Therefore we must not look upon our own, but upon our brother's powers, so that he who is weak in faith, and attempts to follow the strong, may not be destroyed of the devil. Therefore, dear brethren, follow me; I have never been a destroyer. And I was also the very first whom God called to this work. I cannot run away, but will remain as long as God allows. I was also the one to whom God first revealed that his Word should be preached to you. I am also sure that you have the pure Word of God.

Let us, therefore, let us act with fear and humility, cast ourselves at one another's feet, join hands with each other, and help one another. I will do my part, which is no more than my duty, for I love you even as I love my own soul. For here we battle not against pope or bishop, but against the devil [cf. Eph. 6:12], and do you imagine he is asleep? He sleeps not, but sees the true light rising, and to keep it from shining into his eyes he would like to make a flank attack—and he will succeed, if we are not on our guard.

1. Luther is thinking of such things as changes in the eucharistic service and the removal of images (see above, p. 16).

I know him well, and I hope, too, that with the help of God, I am his master. But if we yield him but an inch, we must soon look to it how we may be rid of him. Therefore all those have erred who have helped and consented to abolish the mass; not that it was not a good thing, but that it was not done in an orderly way.[2] You say it was right according to the Scriptures. I agree, but what becomes of order? For it was done in wantonness, with no regard for proper order and with offense to your neighbor. If, beforehand, you had called upon God in earnest prayer, and had obtained the aid of the authorities, one could be certain that it had come from God. I, too, would have taken steps toward the same end if it had been a good thing to do; and if the mass were not so evil a thing, I would introduce it again. For I cannot defend your action, as I have just said. To the papists and blockheads I could defend it, for I could say: How do you know whether it was done with good or bad intention, since the work in itself was really a good work? But I would not know what to assert before the devil. For if on their deathbeds the devil reminds those who began this affair of texts like these, "Every plant which my Father has not planted will be rooted up" [Matt. 15:13], or "I have not sent them, yet they ran" [Jer. 23:21], how will they be able to withstand? He will cast them into hell. But I shall poke the one spear into his face, so that even the world will become too small for him, for I know that in spite of my reluctance I was called by the council to preach. Therefore I was willing to accept you as you were willing to accept me, and, besides, you could have consulted me about the matter.

I was not so far away that you could not reach me with a letter, whereas not the slightest communication was sent to me. If you were going to begin something and make me responsible for it, that would have been too hard. I will not do it [i.e., assume the responsibility]. Here one can see that you do not have the Spirit, even though you do have a deep knowledge of the Scriptures. Take note of these two things, "must" and "free." The "must" is that which necessity requires, and which must ever be unyielding; as, for instance, the faith, which I shall never permit anyone to take away from me, but must always keep in my heart and freely confess before

2. Karlstadt celebrated the first public evangelical Eucharist in defiance of the elector and without any governmental approval (see above, pp. 5–6). But the Wittenberg city government took official action incorporating these changes in January 1522 (see above, p. 16).

everyone. But "free" is that in which I have choice, and may use or not, yet in such a way that it profit my brother and not me. Now do not make a "must" out of what is "free," as you have done, so that you may not be called to account for those who were led astray by your loveless exercise of liberty. For if you entice anyone to eat meat on Friday, and he is troubled about it on his deathbed, and thinks, Woe is me, for I have eaten meat and I am lost! God will call you to account for that soul. I, too, would like to begin many things, in which but few would follow me, but what is the use? For I know that, when it comes to the showdown, those who have begun this thing cannot maintain themselves, and will be the first to retreat. How would it be, if I brought the people to the point of attack, and though I had been the first to exhort others, I would then flee, and not face death with courage? How the poor people would be deceived!

Let us, therefore, feed others also with the milk which we received, until they, too, become strong in faith. For there are many who are otherwise in accord with us and who would also gladly accept this thing, but they do not yet fully understand it—these we drive away. Therefore, let us show love to our neighbors; if we do not do this, our work will not endure. We must have patience with them for a time, and not cast out him who is weak in faith; and do and omit to do many other things, so long as love requires it and it does no harm to our faith. If we do not earnestly pray to God and act rightly in this matter, it looks to me as if all the misery which we have begun to heap upon the papists will fall upon us. Therefore I could no longer remain away, but was compelled to come and say these things to you.

This is enough about the mass; tomorrow we shall speak about images.

The Second Sermon, March 10, 1522, Monday after Invocavit

Dear friends, you heard yesterday the chief characteristics of a Christian man, that his whole life and being is faith and love. Faith is directed toward God, love toward man and one's neighbor, and consists in such love and service for him as we have received from

God without our work and merit. Thus, there are two things: the one, which is the most needful, and which must be done in one way and no other; the other, which is a matter of choice and not of necessity, which may be kept or not, without endangering faith or incurring hell. In both, love must deal with our neighbor in the same manner as God has dealt with us; it must walk the straight road, straying neither to the left nor to the right. In the things which are "musts" and are matters of necessity, such as believing in Christ, love nevertheless never uses force or undue constraint. Thus the mass is an evil thing, and God is displeased with it, because it is performed as if it were a sacrifice and work of merit. Therefore it must be abolished. Here there can be no question or doubt, any more than you should ask whether you should worship God. Here we are entirely agreed: the private masses must be abolished. As I have said in my writings,[3] I wish they would be abolished everywhere and only the ordinary evangelical mass be retained. Yet Christian love should not employ harshness here nor force the matter. However, it should be preached and taught with tongue and pen that to hold mass in such a manner is sinful, and yet no one should be dragged away from it by the hair; for it should be left to God, and his Word should be allowed to work alone, without our work or interference. Why? Because it is not in my power or hand to fashion the hearts of men as the potter molds the clay and fashion them at my pleasure [Ecclus. 33:13]. I can get no farther than their ears; their hearts I cannot reach. And since I cannot pour faith into their hearts, I cannot, nor should I, force any one to have faith. That is God's work alone, who causes faith to live in the heart. Therefore we should give free course to the Word and not add our works to it. We have the *jus verbi* [right to speak] but not the *executio* [power to accomplish]. We should preach the Word, but the results must be left solely to God's good pleasure.

Now if I should rush in and abolish it by force, there are many who would be compelled to consent to it and yet not know where they stand, whether it is right or wrong, and they would say: I do not know if it is right or wrong, I do not know where I stand, I was compelled by force to submit to the majority. And this forcing and commanding results in a mere mockery, an external show, a fool's

3. See *To the Christian Nobility of the German Nation* (1520), *LW* 44, 123–217 and *The Babylonian Captivity of the Church*, *LW* 36, 18–57.

play, man-made ordinances, sham-saints, and hypocrites. For where the heart is not good, I care nothing at all for the work. We must first win the hearts of the people. But that is done when I teach only the Word of God, preach the gospel, and say: Dear lords or pastors, abandon the mass, it is not right, you are sinning when you do it; I cannot refrain from telling you this. But I would not make it an ordinance for them, nor urge a general law. He who would follow me could do so, and he who refused would remain outside. In the latter case the Word would sink into the heart and do its work. Thus he would become convinced and acknowledge his error, and fall away from the mass; tomorrow another would do the same, and thus God would accomplish more with his Word than if you and I were to merge all our power into one heap. So when you have won the heart, you have won the man—and thus the thing must finally fall of its own weight and come to an end. And if the hearts and minds of all are agreed and united, abolish it. But if all are not heart and soul for its abolishment—leave it in God's hands, I beseech you, otherwise the result will not be good. Not that I would again set up the mass; I let it lie in God's name. Faith must not be chained and imprisoned, nor bound by an ordinance to any work. This is the principle by which you must be governed. For I am sure you will not be able to carry out your plans. And if you should carry them out with such general laws, then I will recant everything that I have written and preached and I will not support you. This I am telling you now. What harm can it do you? You still have your faith in God, pure and strong so that this thing cannot hurt you.

Love, therefore, demands that you have compassion on the weak, as all the apostles had. Once, when Paul came to Athens (Acts 17 [:16-32]), a mighty city, he found in the temple many ancient altars, and he went from one to the other and looked at them all, but he did not kick down a single one of them with his foot. Rather he stood up in the middle of the market place and said they were nothing but idolatrous things and begged the people to forsake them; yet he did not destroy one of them by force. When the Word took hold of their hearts, they forsook them of their own accord, and in consequence the thing fell of itself. Likewise, if I had seen them holding mass, I would have preached to them and admonished them. Had they heeded my admonition, I would have won them; if not, I would nevertheless not have torn them from it by the hair or employed any force, but simply allowed the Word to act and prayed for them. For the Word created heaven and earth and all things [Ps. 33:6]; the Word must do this thing, and not we poor sinners.

In short, I will preach it, teach it, write it, but I will constrain no man by force, for faith must come freely without compulsion. Take myself as an example. I opposed indulgences and all the papists, but never with force. I simply taught, preached, and wrote God's Word; otherwise I did nothing. And while I slept [cf. Mark 4:26-29], or drank Wittenberg beer with my friends Philip[4] and Amsdorf,[5] the Word so greatly weakened the papacy that no prince or emperor ever inflicted such losses upon it. I did nothing; the Word did everything. Had I desired to foment trouble, I could have brought great bloodshed upon Germany; indeed, I could have started such a game that even the emperor would not have been safe. But what would it have been? Mere fool's play. I did nothing; I let the Word do its work. What do you suppose is Satan's thought when one tries to do the thing by kicking up a row? He sits back in hell and thinks: Oh, what a fine game the poor fools are up to now! But when we spread the Word alone and let it alone do the work, that distresses him. For it is almighty and takes captive the hearts, and when the hearts are captured the work will fall of itself. Let me cite a simple instance. In former times there were sects, too, Jewish and Gentile Christians, differing on the law of Moses with respect to circumcision. The former wanted to keep it, the latter not. Then came Paul and preached that it might be kept or not, for it was of no consequence, and also that they should not make a "must" of it, but leave it to the choice of the individual; to keep it or not was immaterial [I Cor. 7:18-24; Gal. 5:1]. So it was up to the time of Jerome,[6] who came and wanted to make a "must" out of it, desiring to make it an ordinance and a law that it be prohibited. Then came St. Augustine and he was of the same opinion as St. Paul: it might be kept or not, as one wished. St. Jerome was a hundred miles away from St. Paul's opinion. The two doctors

4. Philip Melanchthon (1497–1560), professor at Wittenberg.

5. Nicholas von Amsdorf (1483–1565).

6. Jerome (c. 345–420) created the Latin translation of the Bible (the Vulgate).

bumped heads rather hard, but when St. Augustine died, St. Jerome was successful in having it prohibited. After that came the popes, who also wanted to add something and they, too, made laws. Thus out of the making of one law grew a thousand laws, until they have completely buried us under laws. And this is what will happen here, too; one law will soon make two, two will increase to three, and so forth.

Let this be enough at this time concerning the things that are necessary, and let us beware lest we lead astray those of weak conscience [I Cor. 8:12].

The Third Sermon, March 11, 1522, Tuesday after Invocavit

Concerning Images[7]

But now we must come to the images, and concerning them also it is true that they are unnecessary, and we are free to have them or not, although it would be much better if we did not have them at all. I am not partial to them. A great controversy arose on the subject of images[8] between the Roman emperor and the pope; the emperor held that he had the authority to banish the images, but the pope insisted that they should remain, and both were wrong. Much blood was shed, but the pope emerged as victor and the emperor lost. What was it all about? They wished to make a "must" out of that which is free. This God cannot tolerate. Do you presume to do things differently from the way the supreme Majesty

7. On January 27, 1522, Karlstadt published a widely influential tract on images, *Von abtuhung der Bylder*, reprinted in Hans Lietzmann, ed., *Andreas Karlstadt: Von Abtuhung der Bilder* ("Kleine Texte fur theologische und philologische Vorlesungen und Übungen," No. 74; Bonn, 1911). Karlstadt argued that images must be removed because the first commandment (Exod. 20:4), he believed, explicitly forbade images. He also realized that popular piety had in fact become idolatrous in its attitude toward images (pp. 13–14, 17–19). Karlstadt explicitly called on the highest governmental authorities (i.e., the Wittenberg city council to remove the images) (pp. 20–21).

8. The Iconoclastic Controversy initiated by Emperor Leo III in 718 was finally settled in 843.

has decreed? Surely not; let it alone. You read in the law (Exod. 20 [:4]), "You shall not make yourself a graven image, or any likeness of anything that is in heaven above, or that is in the earth beneath, or that is in the water under the earth." There you take your stand; that is your ground. Now let us see! When our adversaries say: The meaning of the first commandment is that we should worship only one God and not any image, even as it is said immediately following, "You shall not bow down to them or serve them" [Exod. 20:5], and when they say that it is the worship of images which is forbidden and not the making of them, they are shaking our foundation and making it uncertain. And if you reply: The text says, "You shall not make any images," then they say: It also says, "You shall not worship them." In the face of such uncertainty who would be so bold as to destroy the images? Not I. But let us go further. They say: Did not Noah, Abraham, Jacob build altars? [Gen. 8:20; 12:7; 13:4; 13:18; 33:20]. And who will deny that? We must admit it. Again, did not Moses erect a bronze serpent, as we read in his fourth book (Num. 22 [21:9])? How then can you say that Moses forbade the making of images when he himself made one? It seems to me that such a serpent is an image, too. How shall we answer that? Again, do we not read also that two birds were erected on the mercy seat [Exod. 37:7], the very place where God willed that he should be worshipped? Here we must admit that we may have images and make images, but we must not worship them, and if they are worshipped, they should be put away and destroyed, just as King Hezekiah broke in pieces the bronze serpent erected by Moses [II Kings 18:4]. And who will be so bold as to say, when he is challenged to give an answer: They worship the images. They will say: Are you the man who dares to accuse us of worshipping them? Do not believe that they will acknowledge it. To be sure, it is true, but we cannot make them admit it. Just look how they acted when I condemned works without faith. They said: Do you believe that we have no faith, or that our works are performed without faith? Then I cannot press them any further, but must put my flute back in my pocket; for if they gain a hair's breadth, they make a hundred miles out of it.

Therefore it should have been preached that images were nothing and that no service is done to God by erecting them; then they would have fallen of themselves. That is what I did; that is what Paul did in Athens, when he went into their churches and saw all their idols. He did not strike at any of them, but stood in the market place and said, "You men of Athens, you are all idolatrous" [Acts 17:16, 22]. He preached against their idols, but he overthrew none by force. And you rush, create an uproar, break down altars, and overthrow images![9] Do you really believe you can abolish the altars in this way? No, you will only set them up more firmly. Even if you overthrew the images in this place, do you think you have overthrown those in Nürnberg and the rest of the world? Not at all. St. Paul, as we read in the Book of Acts [28:11], sat in a ship on whose prow were painted or carved the Twin Brothers [i.e., Castor and Pollux]. He went on board and did not bother about them at all, neither did he break them off. Why must Luke describe the Twins at this point? Without doubt he wanted to show that outward things could do no harm to faith, if only the heart does not cleave to them or put its trust in them. This is what we must preach and teach, and let the Word alone do the work, as I said before. The Word must first capture the hearts of men and enlighten them; we will not be the ones who will do it. Therefore the apostles magnified their ministry, *ministerium* [Rom. 11:13], and not its effect, *executio*.

Let this be enough for today.

The Fourth Sermon, March 12, 1522, Wednesday after Invocavit

Dear friends, we have now heard about the things which are "musts," such as that the mass is not to be observed as a sacrifice. Then we considered the things which are not necessary but free, such as marriage, the monastic life, and the abolishing of images. We have treated these four subjects, and have said that in all these matters love is the captain. On the subject of images, in particular, we saw that they ought to be abolished when they are worshipped;

9. For a contemporary report of the disorderly crowd that destroyed the images, see *WB*, No. 92, p. 191 and No. 93, p. 195. For Karlstadt's opposition to disorder, see above, the note on p. 16, and p. 25, n. 7.

otherwise not—although because of the abuses they give rise to, I wish they were everywhere abolished. This cannot be denied. For whoever places an image in a church imagines he has performed a service to God and done a good work, which is downright idolatry. But this, the greatest, foremost, and highest reason for abolishing images, you have passed by, and fastened on the least important reason of all. For I suppose there is nobody, or certainly very few, who do not understand that yonder crucifix is not my God, for my God is in heaven, but that this is simply a sign. But the world is full of that other abuse; for who would place a silver or wooden image in a church unless he thought that by so doing he was rendering God a service? Do you think that Duke Frederick, the bishop of Halle,[10] and the others would have dragged so many silver images into the churches, if they thought it counted for nothing before God? No, they would not bother to do it. But this is not sufficient reason to abolish, destroy, and burn all images. Why? Because we must admit that there are still some people who hold no such wrong opinion of them, but to whom they may well be useful, although they are few. Nevertheless, we cannot and ought not to condemn a thing which may be any way useful to a person. You should rather have taught that images are nothing, that God cares nothing for them, and that he is not served nor pleased when we make an image for him, but that we would do better to give a poor man a gold-piece than God a golden image; for God has forbidden the latter, but not the former. If they had heard this teaching that images count for nothing, they would have ceased of their own accord, and the images would have fallen without any uproar or tumult, as they are already beginning to do.

We must, therefore, be on our guard, for the devil, through his apostles, is after us with all his craft and cunning. Now, although it is true and no one can deny that the images are evil because they are abused, nevertheless we must not on that account reject them, nor condemn anything because it is abused. This would result in utter confusion. God has commanded us in Deut. 4 [:19] not to lift up our eyes to the sun [and the moon and the stars], etc., that we may not worship them, for they are created to serve all nations. But

10. Duke Frederick is Elector Frederick the Wise of Saxony (1463-1525). The "bishop of Halle" is probably Albrecht of Hohenzollern, archbishop of Mainz and of Magdeburg (*LW* 51, 84, n. 19).

there are many people who worship the sun and the stars. Therefore we propose to rush in and pull the sun and stars from the skies. No, we had better let it be. Again, wine and women bring many a man to misery and make a fool of him [Ecclus. 19:2; 31:30]; so we kill all the women and pour out all the wine. Again, gold and silver cause much evil, so we condemn them. Indeed, if we want to drive away our worst enemy, the one who does us the most harm, we shall have to kill ourselves, for we have no greater enemy than our own heart, as the prophet, Jer. 17 [:9], says, "The heart of man is crooked," or, as I take the meaning, "always twisting to one side." And so on—what would we not do?

He who would blacken the devil must have good charcoal, for he, too, wears fine clothes and is invited to the kermis.[11] But I can catch him by asking him: Do you not place the images in the churches because you think it a special service to God? And when he says Yes, as he must, you may conclude that what was meant as a service of God he has turned into idolatry by abusing the images and practicing what God has not commanded. But he has neglected God's command, which is that he should be helpful to his neighbor. But I have not yet caught him, though actually he is caught and will not admit it; he escapes me by saying: Yes, I help the poor, too; cannot I give to my neighbor and at the same time donate images? This is not so, however, for who would not rather give his neighbor a gold-piece than God a golden image? No, he would not trouble himself about placing images in churches if he did not believe, as he actually does, that he was doing God a service. Therefore I must admit that images are neither here nor there, neither evil nor good, we may have them or not, as we please. This trouble has been caused by you; the devil would not have accomplished it with me, for I cannot deny that it is possible to find someone to whom images are useful. And if I were asked about it, I would confess that none of these things gives offense to one, and if just one man were found on earth who used the images aright, the devil would soon draw the conclusion against me: Why, then, do you condemn what may be used properly? Then he has gained the offensive and I would have to admit it. He would not have got nearly so far if I

11. *Kirchmess*: service for the consecration or commemoration of the consecration of a church, an occasion for placing images or embellishments in the church (*LW* 51, 85, n. 20).

had been here. Proudly he scattered us, though it has done no harm to the Word of God. You wanted to blacken the devil, but you forgot the charcoal and used chalk. If you want to fight the devil you must know the Scriptures well and, besides, use them at the right time.

Concerning Meats

Let us proceed and speak of the eating of meats and what our attitude should be in this matter. It is true that we are free to eat any kind of food, meats, fish, eggs, or butter. This no one can deny. God has given us this liberty; this is true. Nevertheless, we must know how to use our liberty, and in this matter treat the weak brother quite differently from the stubborn. Observe, then, how you ought to use this liberty.

First, if you cannot abstain from meat without harm to yourself, or if you are sick, you may eat whatever you like, and if anyone takes offense, let him be offended. Even if the whole world took offense, you are not committing a sin, for God can approve it in view of the liberty he has so graciously bestowed upon you and of the necessities of your health, which would be endangered by your abstinence.

Secondly, if you should be pressed to eat fish instead of meat on Friday, and to eat fish and abstain from eggs and butter during Lent, etc., as the pope has done with his fool's laws, then you must in no wise allow yourself to be drawn away from the liberty in which God has placed you, but do just the contrary to spite him, and say: Because you forbid me to eat meat and presume to turn my liberty into law, I will eat meat in spite of you. And thus you must do in all other things which are matters of liberty. To give you an example: if the pope, or anyone else, were to force me to wear a cowl, just as he prescribes it, I would take off the cowl just to spite him. But since it is left to my own free choice, I wear it or take it off, according to my pleasure.

Thirdly, there are some who are still weak in faith, who ought to be instructed, and who would gladly believe as we do. But their ignorance prevents them, and if this were preached to them, as it was to us, they would be one with us. Toward such well-meaning people we must assume an entirely different attitude from that which we assume toward the stubborn. We must bear patiently with these people and not use our liberty; since it brings no peril or harm to body or soul; in fact, it is rather salutary, and we are doing our brothers and sisters a great service besides. But if we use our liberty unnecessarily, and deliberately cause offense to our neighbor, we drive away the very one who in time would come to our faith. Thus St. Paul circumcised Timothy [Acts 16:3] because simple-minded Jews had taken offense; he thought: What harm can it do, since they are offended because of their ignorance? But when, in Antioch, they insisted that he ought and must circumcise Titus [Gal. 2:3], Paul withstood them all and to spite them refused to have Titus circumcised [Gal. 2:11]. And he stood his ground. He did the same when St. Peter by the exercise of his liberty caused a wrong conception in the minds of the unlearned. It happened in this way: when Peter was with the Gentiles, he ate pork and sausages with them, but when the Jews came in, he abstained from this food and did not eat as he did before. Then the Gentiles who had become Christians thought: Alas! we, too, must be like the Jews, eat no pork, and live according to the law of Moses. But when Paul learned that they were acting to the injury of evangelical freedom, he reproved Peter publicly and read him an apostolic lecture, saying: "If you, though a Jew, live like a Gentile, how can you compel the Gentiles to live like Jews?" [Gal. 2:14]. Thus we, too, should order our lives and use our liberty at the proper time, so that Christian liberty may suffer no injury, and no offense be given to our weak brothers and sisters who are still without the knowledge of this liberty.

The Fifth Sermon, March 13, 1522, Thursday after Invocavit

. . . Let us now consider how we must observe the blessed sacrament.

You have heard how I preached[12] against the foolish law of the pope and opposed his precept, that no woman shall wash the altar linen on which the body of Christ has lain, even if it be a pure nun, except it first be washed by a pure priest. . . .

Against such fool laws we have preached and exposed them, in order that it might be made known that no sin is involved in these

12. See *On the Abuse of the Mass* (1521); *WA* 8, 477–563, esp. pp. 508, 540 (*LW* 51, 88, n. 22).

foolish laws and commandments of the pope, and that a layman does not commit sin if he touches the cup or the body of Christ with his hands. You should give thanks to God that you have come to such clear knowledge, which many great men have lacked. But now you go ahead and become as foolish as the pope, in that you think that a person must touch the sacrament with his hands.[13] You want to prove that you are good Christians by touching the sacrament with your hands, and thus you have dealt with the sacrament, which is our highest treasure, in such a way that it is a wonder you were not struck to the ground by thunder and lightning. All the other things God might have suffered, but this he cannot allow, because you have made a compulsion of it. And if you do not stop this, neither the emperor nor anyone else need drive me from you, I will go without urging; and I dare say that none of my enemies, though they have caused me much sorrow, have wounded me as you have.

If you want to show that you are good Christians by handling the sacrament and boast of it before the world, then Herod and Pilate are the chief and best Christians, since it seems to me that they really handled the body of Christ when they had him nailed to the cross and put to death. No, my dear friends, the kingdom of God does not consist in outward things, which can be touched or perceived, but in faith [Luke 17:20; Rom. 14:17; I Cor. 4:20].

But you may say: We live and we ought to live according to the Scriptures, and God has so instituted the sacrament that we must take it with our hands, for he said, "Take, eat, this is my body" [Matt. 26:26]. The answer is this: though I am convinced beyond a doubt that the disciples of the Lord took it with their hands, and though I admit that you may do the same without committing sin, nevertheless I can neither make it compulsory nor defend it. And my reason is that the devil, when he really pushes us to the wall,

13. Karlstadt allowed each person to take the sacrament in his own hands at the first evangelical Eucharist on Christmas day (see above, pp. 5–6). (For a discussion of the relationship between the laity's handling the sacrament and the priesthood of believers, see below, pp. 155–56). The council decree of January 24, 1521, stated that the communicant would take the sacrament in his own hands (*ABK*-S, p. 166). In the case of receiving both kinds, however, the decree of January 24 allowed the communicant to receive either one or both elements. Thus it gave more freedom to the average person than did Luther who demanded a return to the medieval practice where the laity could only receive the bread. See *WM*, pp. 78ff. for the interesting suggestion that when Luther's "rhetoric of evangelical liberty was translated into reality," it meant liberty for the leaders but not for the congregation.

will argue: Where have you read in the Scriptures that "take" means "grasping with the hands"? How, then, am I going to prove or defend it? Indeed, how will I answer him when he cites from the Scriptures the very opposite, and proves that "take" does not mean to receive with the hands only, but also to convey to ourselves in other ways? "Listen to this, my good fellow," he will say, "is not the word 'take' used by three evangelists when they described the Lord's taking of gall and vinegar? [Matt. 27:34; Mark 15:23; Luke 23:36]. You must admit that the Lord did not touch or handle it with his hands, for his hands were nailed to the cross." This verse is a strong argument against me. Again, he cites the passage: *Et accepit omnes timor,* "Fear seized them all" [Luke 7:16], where again we must admit that fear has no hands. Thus I am driven into a corner and must concede, even against my will, that "take" means not only to receive with the hands, but to convey to myself in any other way in which it can be done. Therefore, dear friends, we must be on firm ground, if we are to withstand the devil's attack [Eph. 6:11]. Although I must acknowledge that you committed no sin when you touched the sacrament with your hands, nevertheless I must tell you that it was not a good work, because it caused offense everywhere. For the universal custom is to receive the blessed sacrament from the hands of the priest. Why will you not in this respect also serve those who are weak in faith and abstain from your liberty, particularly since it does not help you if you do it, nor harm you if you do not do it.

Therefore no new practices should be introduced, unless the gospel has first been thoroughly preached and understood, as it has been among you. On this account, dear friends, let us deal soberly and wisely in the things that pertain to God, for God will not be mocked [Gal. 6:7]. The saints may endure mockery, but with God it is vastly different. Therefore, I beseech you, give up this practice.

. . . .

The Eighth Sermon, March 16, 1522, Reminiscere Sunday

A Short Summary of the Sermon of D[r.] M[artin] L[uther] Preached on Reminiscere Sunday on Private Confession

Now we have heard all the things which ought to be considered here, except confession.[14] Of this we shall speak now.

In the first place, there is a confession which is founded on the Scriptures, and it is this: when anybody committed a sin publicly or with other men's knowledge, he was accused before the congregation. If he abandoned his sin, they interceded for him with God. But if he would not listen to the congregation [*häuffen*], he was cast out and excluded from the assembly, so that no one would have anything to do with him. And this confession is commanded by God in Matt. 18 [:15], "If your brother sins against you (so that you and others are offended), go and tell him his fault, between you and him alone." We no longer have any trace of this kind of confession any more; at this point the gospel is in abeyance. Anybody who was able to re-establish it would be doing a good work. Here is where you should have exerted yourselves and re-established this kind of confession, and let the other things go; for no one would have been offended by this and everything would have gone smoothly and quietly. It should be done in this way: When you see a usurer, adulterer, thief, or drunkard, you should go to him in secret, and admonish him to give up his sin. If he will not listen, you should take two others with you and admonish him once more, in a brotherly way, to give up his sin. But if he scorns that, you should tell the pastor before the whole congregation, have your witnesses with you, and accuse him before the pastor in the presence of the people, saying: Dear pastor, this man has done this and that and would not take our brotherly admonition to give up his sin. Therefore I accuse him, together with my witnesses, who have heard this. Then, if he will not give up and willingly acknowledge his guilt, the pastor should exclude him and put him under the ban before the whole assembly, for the sake of the congregation, until he comes to himself and is received back again. This would be Christian. But I cannot undertake to carry it out single-handed.

Secondly, we need a kind of confession when we go into a corner by ourselves and confess to God himself and pour out before him all our faults. This kind of confession is also commanded. . . .

Thirdly, there is also the kind of confession in which one takes another aside and tells him what troubles one, so that one may hear

14. This sermon was prompted by Karlstadt's sermon of December 25, 1521 (see chap. 1).

from him a word of comfort; and this confession is commanded by the pope. It is this urging and forcing which I condemned when I wrote concerning confession,[15] and I refuse to go to confession simply because the pope has commanded it and insists upon it. For I wish him to keep his hands off the confession and not make of it a compulsion or command, which he has not the power to do. Nevertheless I will allow no man to take private confession away from me, and I would not give it up for all the treasures in the world, since I know what comfort and strength it has given me. No one knows what it can do for him except one who has struggled often and long with the devil. Yea, the devil would have slain me long ago, if the confession had not sustained me. For there are many doubtful matters which a man cannot resolve or find the answer to by himself, and so he takes his brother aside and tells him his trouble. What harm is there if he humbles himself a little before his neighbor, puts himself to shame, looks for a word of comfort from him, accepts it, and believes it, as if he were hearing it from God himself, as we read in Matt. 18 [:19], "If two of you agree about anything they ask, it will be done for them."

Moreover, we must have many absolutions, so that we may strengthen our timid consciences and despairing hearts against the devil and against God. Therefore, no man shall forbid the confession nor keep or draw anyone away from it. And if anyone is wrestling with his sins and wants to be rid of them and desires a sure word on the matter, let him go and confess to another in secret, and accept what he says to him as if God himself had spoken it through the mouth of this person. However, one who has a strong, firm faith that his sins are forgiven may let this confession go and confess to God alone. But how many have such a strong faith? Therefore, as I have said, I will not let this private confession be taken from me. But I will not have anybody forced to it, but left to each one's free will.

. . . .

15. *Von der Beichte, ob die der Papst Macht habe zu gebieten* (1521), *WA* 8, 138–204 (*LW* 51, 98, n. 31).

3

Confrontation at the Black Bear

Eclipsed and disgraced after Luther's powerful sermons of March 1522 (see chap. 2), Karlstadt moved in 1523 to Orlamünde, a town in Thuringia, where he was able to introduce the innovations which had been squelched at Wittenberg. During these years, Karlstadt also came to know Thomas Müntzer, preacher at Allstedt in Thuringia. Their contacts however, were very limited* and Karlstadt was strongly opposed to Müntzer's program of violent revolution.†

Since early in 1524, Luther had complained to the princes about Karlstadt's activity in Orlamünde. He objected to the books Karlstadt was publishing (even though they contained no direct attack on Luther). He must also have known about and strongly disapproved of Karlstadt's rejection of the traditional doctrine of the Real Presence in the Eucharist. In order to remove Karlstadt from Orlamünde, the University of Wittenberg tried to force him to return to the university in mid-1524. Instead, Karlstadt resigned his archdeaconate in July and stayed on in Orlamünde.

In August 1524, the princes of Saxony sent Martin Luther on an official visitation of the churches of Thuringia. They hoped that his visit would avoid threatened rebellion and squelch suspected heresy. By the time Luther began his tour, the revolutionary

* Karlstadt wrote a friendly, critical letter to Müntzer on December 21, 1522, and invited him to visit (Günther Franz, ed., *Thomas Müntzer: Schriften und Briefe* [Gütersloh: Gütersloher Verlagshaus Gerd Mohn, 1968], pp. 386–87). But this letter did not lead to a close acquaintance. In a letter to Luther of July 9, 1523, Müntzer asked Luther to greet "Philip, Karlstadt . . . and the others *in your church*" [my italics]; ibid., pp. 391–92. Three weeks later, Müntzer wrote to Karlstadt complaining of his total ignorance of Karlstadt who had failed to write (ibid., p. 393).

† See below, p. 41, n. 9.

Thomas Müntzer, who had been plotting armed rebellion for months at Allstedt, had fled. But Karlstadt was still in Orlamünde.

When Luther came to preach at Jena on August 22, he invaded turf friendly to Karlstadt. A number of Karlstadt's books had been printed there within the past ten months. Martin Reinhard, the preacher at Jena, was a close personal friend of Karlstadt. With a hat pulled over his face to avoid recognition, Karlstadt listened to Luther's blistering sermonic attack on the demonic spirit that provokes rebellion and destroys images. Stung, Karlstadt promptly penned a sharp letter to Luther, requesting an interview. The result was the dramatic confrontation at the Black Bear.

The *Acta Jenensia,* as the anonymous account of the historic encounter is called, was prepared very soon after the event (Luther saw a copy by October 3). The author was clearly sympathetic to Karlstadt. Nonetheless, as the editors of the critical edition of Luther's works observe, it appears to be an essentially accurate record of what transpired.*

For further discussion of the historical background and the debate, see below, pp. 150–57; Gordon Rupp, *Patterns of Reformation* (Philadelphia: Fortress, 1969), pp. 131ff.; *ABK*-B, pp. 124ff.; *ABK*-S, pp. 174–201; *WA* 15, 323–30. A modern German text is in *St. L.* 15, 2028ff. The translation is from the German text in *WA* 15, 334–40.

* See *WA* 15, 327. Luther's subsequent references to the encounter at Jena reflected somewhat different recollections (see, for example, below, pp. 105, 111; also *LW* 40, 69, 136, 186). For a later recollection by Karlstadt, see his letter of September 11, 1524, in Hertzsch 2, 53–54.

What Dr. Andreas Bodenstein von Karlstadt Talked Over with Dr. Martin Luther at Jena, and How They Have Decided to Write against Each Other

1524

In [334] the fifteen hundred and twenty-fourth year after the birth of Christ, on Monday the eighth day after our Lady's ascension, which is the twenty-second of August, the highly learned, etc. Martin Luther, doctor of Holy Scripture, after he had arrived on the previous Sunday afternoon at Jena to preach there and elsewhere according to the princely command of the illustrious, right honorable princes and lords, the dukes of Saxony, etc.—the aforesaid Dr. Martin began to preach early around seven o'clock on the aforesaid day and preached one and one-half hours concerning and against the doctrine and fruit of the spirits. Among others, he named the spirit at Allstedt,[1] and related some fruits such as riot and murder which indeed have previously almost occurred at Zwickau[2] by the same spirit as one of his lofty fruits.

He said it would be equally the work and fruit of this spirit to tear down churches, images, wood and stone, and in short to take away, to root out and completely bring to naught baptism and the sacrament of the altar, as indeed this spirit of Allstedt has even undertaken here and there much more by the same inspiration of a demonic spirit.[3] In summary, he said that a demonic spirit performs

1. Allstedt was the town where Thomas Müntzer was preaching and organizing armed revolution in the spring and summer of 1524. On Müntzer, see Eric W. Gritsch, *Reformer without a Church: The Life and Thought of Thomas Muentzer* (Philadelphia: Fortress, 1967) and Gordon Rupp, *Patterns of Reformation* (Philadelphia: Fortress, 1969), pp. 157–353.

2. Earlier, in 1520–21, Müntzer had sparked riotous disorder and possibly an attempt at civic revolution while serving as preacher at Zwickau.

3. Luther is apparently attacking Karlstadt here because Karlstadt, although opposed to violence, had promoted the orderly removal of images, abandoned the doctrine of the Real Presence in the Eucharist, and probably suspended infant baptism at Orlamünde. See *ABK*-S, pp. 188–89.

all these fruit. In order that the elect would not be frightened, however, Dr. Luther comforted them in the sermon and said: They are not many, although they are many. Nevertheless they must indeed increase and form sects so that the elect are proved true and the godless are disgraced. We, however, he said, have previously passed judgment on them, as the sermons[4] further indicate, and can still by God's grace judge that he who undertakes such things is not a good spirit but rather the devil himself.

When Dr. Karlstadt heard these and similar words in the sermon (for he himself was in the service), he took them to heart. He found that he was hit by some things, as will be shown below. He wrote a letter[5] to Dr. Luther [335] which some in the aforesaid Inn of the Black Bear read over the noon meal. Karlstadt wrote that if Dr. Luther were not opposed, he would gladly speak with him. At that, Dr. Luther gave an oral answer to Dr. Karlstadt's envoy: If Dr. Karlstadt would like to come to him, he could certainly permit it; if not, he could certainly forgo it.

After this, Dr. Karlstadt dispatched someone to Dr. Luther once more to say that if it were convenient for him, he would like to come. Luther answered: In the name of God, he may come if he wishes; I am ready. When Dr. Karlstadt was informed of this, he came and Dr. Gerhard Westerburg[6] came with him. In the inn, there were also many unfamiliar messengers of the emperor and margrave as well as very many people from Jena who listened to this discussion and took great pleasure from it although it terrified some of the timid, and greatly amazed many. Karlstadt had one of the servants notify Dr. Martin that he was there and would like to speak with him. Dr. Martin answered: He should come in here and freely negotiate with me in public. That happened thus, and the discussion followed as it stands here.

And so Karlstadt entered the room, at the bidding of Dr. Martin sat on a chair opposite him and his other companions at the table, and began to speak in this way:

KARLSTADT: Dear Mr. Doctor and all you dear brothers, I pray that you will not take offense at my importuning you here. My

4. Luther's Eight Sermons of March 1522; see chap. 2 above.

5. This letter is not extant.

6. Gerhard Westerburg was a disciple and brother-in-law of Karlstadt. See *ABK*-B 2, 17ff., 205–6, 216–17.

innocence and great need compel me. For today in your sermon, Mr. Doctor, you attacked me somewhat severely and you interwove me in one number and work with the riotous murdering spirits, as you call them. I say "No!" to that, although you charge the same spirits with a type of discourse about the living voice of God that I never heard from them in my day.[7] But I do not say that because I want to defend them here. But I speak thus: He who wants to associate me and put me in the same pot with such murdering spirits ascribes that to me without truth and not as an honest man. I know, however, that you had me in mind and that I can apply the things you said to myself because you spoke of the sacrament and attacked me too strongly. I say what I truly know, that is, that no one has written of this in conformity with the apostles in the manner, meaning, and ground as I have. Thus I freely confess that. But I deny that it is a murdering spirit and, as you said today, one and the same spirit as at Allstedt. For he has nothing in common with me in my discussion of the sacrament.

7. For Müntzer's view of the living word, see Gritsch, *Reformer without a Church*, pp. 104, 111–12. Without further information of what Luther said, it is impossible to know if Karlstadt was correct in thinking that Luther distorted Müntzer's position. Luther probably also had the "Zwickau Prophets" in mind in his comment about the living voice of God. Connected with Müntzer in Zwickau in 1521, the Zwickau Prophets fled to Wittenberg at Christmas, 1521. They rejected infant baptism, claimed direct revelation from God apart from the written word, and advocated the use of the sword against the godless. Many historians have claimed that they influenced Karlstadt significantly (e.g., Rupp, *Patterns of Reformation*, pp. 101, 113). But the documents of the Wittenberg Movement demonstrate that it was Melanchthon, not Karlstadt, who was preoccupied with the Zwickau Prophets during their brief stay in Wittenberg (*WB*, No. 59, p. 129; No. 62, p. 135; No. 64, pp. 137ff.; and No. 68, p. 160). Only one document links Karlstadt with them (*WB*, No. 63, p. 136). Furthermore, two of Karlstadt's books written in the period immediately after their stay in Wittenberg contain powerful reaffirmations of *sola scriptura*, and one has a reference to people who belittle biblical authority which is very probably directed against the Zwickau Prophets (*ABK*-S, p. 164). For Karlstadt's most "spiritualist" statement in subsequent years, see below, pp. 74–75 and n. 4 (cf. also p. 97, n. 5). In a recent study, Mark Edwards has pointed out that Luther tended to attribute the views of one set of opponents to all his opponents: "Dominating his *ad hominem* attacks was the conviction that these opponents were motivated by a common satanic spirit. This belief . . . found its most telling expression in his practice of attacking this spirit rather than the opponents themselves, leading him to impute similar characteristics to all his evangelical opponents and to hold any one of them responsible for the views and misdeeds of all" (*Luther and the False Brethren*, pp. 58–59). That was unfortunate for Karlstadt, but it helps explain the dynamics of the encounter at the Black Bear.

At this point, Dr. Martin Luther answered thus:

Dear Mr. Doctor, finally and at the end, I will speak, since you have allowed it. And I say that you can never demonstrate or prove that I named you. But since you [336] assume you are referred to and hit, then be hit in God's name. You have also sent me a sharp letter.[8] You ought not to have done that, for I have nothing to do with you. I am amazed how you accuse yourself. But I see that I have hit you, and I am both glad and sad. I see it gladly because I alone know that you are also one of those concerning whom I preached, as you yourself assume. But I see it without gladness because it pains me that the people should be thus misled. Today I preached against the spirits and I will do it again now. If I hit you, then I hit you.

KARLSTADT: I will also finally begin. I espouse what you said about the sacrament and will prove with Scripture that you have preached the gospel improperly. Moreover, I still say that you treated me violently and improperly by putting me in the same pot with the murdering spirit. I protest publicly before all these brethren assembled together that I having nothing to do with the spirit in the rebellion!

LUTHER: Dear Mr. Doctor, that is not necessary. I have read the letter which you have written to Thomas from Orlamünde and have indeed noticed there that you are against and opposed to rebellion.[9]

KARLSTADT: Why then, Mr. Doctor, have you said that there is just one spirit, that is, the murdering spirit at Allstedt and the spirit which smashes images and attacks the sacrament?[10]

8. See above, p. 39, n. 5.

9. Both Karlstadt and the Orlamünde congregation wrote to Thomas Müntzer rejecting his invitation to join the rebellion. Karlstadt's letter is in Franz, ed., *Müntzer: Schriften und Briefe*, pp. 415–16. The Orlamünde congregation's letter is in E. Hase, "Karlstadt in Orlamünde," *Mitteilungen der Geschichts—und Altertumsforschende Gesellschaft des Osterlandes*, 4 (1858), 108. See also *ABK-S*, pp. 195–96. Luther obviously had seen the letter from Karlstadt's Orlamünde congregation before he traveled throughout Thuringia publicly suggesting that Karlstadt and Müntzer were of the same "spirit." See below, pp. 103–4, for Luther's rationale on a connection between Karlstadt and Münster's call for violence.

10. While admitting that he removes images and denies the Real Presence (and therefore "attacks" or "injures" Luther's view of the sacrament), Karlstadt denies any connection with revolution.

LUTHER: But I named no one. You in particular, I have not named with a single word.

KARLSTADT: I apply it to myself from the context, for I have attacked the present misuse of the sacrament. And I have nothing in common with the spirit of Allstedt in the question of the sacrament. But you preach that there is one murdering and rebellious spirit. But I would indeed like, if I may, to speak with you about what I have written to you.

Then there was a little silence. Karlstadt spoke:

If I had erred and you had wanted to do a Christian work (since you want to be a Christian), then you should have instructed me in a brotherly fashion before you stabbed me publicly. You preach and cry, "Love, love." What kind of love is it when you give alms to some student and see a brother err and do not instruct him?

LUTHER: If I have not preached the gospel correctly, then I do not know it.

KARLSTADT: Yes, I will prove with [your doctrine of] the sacrament how you preached Christ—that is, whether you have preached the crucified Christ or rather a self-invented Christ. You have preached against yourself as it can be read from your books.

LUTHER: Dear Mr. Doctor, if you know that, then write it freely and proceed boldly so that it comes to light.

KARLSTADT: I also want to do that. It must indeed come to light. I do not shrink from the light [337] as you charge me. I offer myself for public disputation at Wittenberg or Erfurt or to hear and receive Christian instruction where and when you desire if only I am given a safe conduct as you have been.[11]

LUTHER: Are you afraid then? Do you not have a safe conduct to Wittenberg?

KARLSTADT: Yes, I was there just now.[12] However, you will not spare me in a public disputation, so I will surely not spare you either. For I know how you have attached the people to yourself.

11. Luther had a safe conduct when he went to the Diet of Worms in 1521; but perhaps Karlstadt refers to Luther's current tour of the Saale Valley, on which Luther was accompanied by at least one representative of the princes.

12. Karlstadt was at Wittenberg to resign his archdeaconate on July 22 (see *ABK*-S, p. 194).

LUTHER: Indeed, dear doctor! No one does anything to you. Just come forward freely.

KARLSTADT: I also want to come to the light. Either I will be disgraced publicly or God's truth will be revealed.

LUTHER: It will happen that your foolishness must be disclosed

KARLSTADT: I will gladly bear the shame so that God retains his honor.

LUTHER: Indeed your [foolishness] will confront you. And I am amazed that you only threaten to write. That frightens no one.

KARLSTADT: Nor am I afraid. I know that my doctrine is correct and from God.

LUTHER: If your doctrine was correct and from God, why then did not your spirit break through when you smashed the images at Wittenberg?[13]

KARLSTADT: I did not undertake that alone. Rather the three councils and some of your companions decided it.[14] Afterward they pulled their heads out of the noose and let me stand alone.

LUTHER: I appeal to them.

KARLSTADT: I do too.

LUTHER: I advise you not to appeal to Wittenberg. Things are not so good there for you as you suppose.

KARLSTADT: Nor do you have it so good as you suppose. But I console myself with truth. At the last day, the day of the Lord will reveal all hidden things. Then one will truly see what each one—even you and I—has done, and nothing will remain hidden under the rug.

LUTHER: You always appeal to the Lord's day, but I desire mercy.

KARLSTADT: Why not? He will not do wrong to anyone or consider the person. The little person will be worth as much as the big person. In this matter, I want to be judged according to mercy and justice. But when you reproach my spirit and say it should be driven away, you finally come to your goal. You bound me hand and foot and then struck me.

13. During the Wittenberg Movement, Karlstadt was accused of fomenting the disorderly action of the rioters who tore down images, but there is no clear evidence that he did so. In his writings, he called on the highest governmental authorities to remove them (see the note on p. 16). See further below, pp. 148–49 and the literature cited there.

14. Especially Melanchthon.

LUTHER: When have I struck you?

KARLSTADT: Was I not bound and struck when you alone wrote, printed, and preached against me and arranged that my books were taken from the press and that I was forbidden to write and preach?[15] If [338] I had been able to write and preach just as freely as you, you would certainly have learned what my spirit would have accomplished.

LUTHER: Why did you want to preach? You were not even called.[16] Who commanded you to preach?

KARLSTADT: If we want to speak of human calling, then I know well that it was my right because of the archdeaconate.[17] And, if we want to speak of God's calling then I also know well what to report about that.

LUTHER: Who commanded you to preach in the parish church?[18]

KARLSTADT: If I had erred there, you should have reproved me in a brotherly way about that beforehand and not have stabbed and struck me thus. Are they not, moreover, the same people who listen in All Saint's Church and in the parish church?

LUTHER: You stabbed me before I stabbed you.

KARLSTADT: I did not do that.

LUTHER: Your books prove that, for you quote my very words.[19]

KARLSTADT: Which book? I have indeed written one recently

15. On Luther's preaching against Karlstadt, see chap. 2 above. Karlstadt was forbidden to preach in early 1522, and the university censors refused to allow his books to be published. See *ABK*-S, pp. 171–75.

16. Luther incorrectly charges Karlstadt with unauthorized preaching during the Wittenberg Movement (see below, n. 18).

17. As archdeacon, Karlstadt was responsible for the preaching at All Saints (*ABK*-S, p. 9), but had no responsibilities at the parish church where Luther preached.

18. Luther apparently did not know that Karlstadt conducted the eucharistic service at the parish church with the consent of the parish minister. But a contemporary report makes this very clear: "Dr. Karlstadt . . . fed the people with bread and wine in the parish church with the consent and assistance of the parish priest [*consenciente ac administrante Parocho*]" *WB*, No. 63, p. 136. There is no clear evidence that he preached in the parish church without authorization (*ABK*-S, pp. 170–71).

19. In none of the eleven books (for the list, see *ABK*-S, p. 202, nn. 3–4) published between March 1522 and this encounter with Luther did Karlstadt attack Luther in any violent way. Only one treatise was directly devoted to the issues over which they had clashed, and this treatise was not violent at all. In the others, Karlstadt was undoubtedly concerned with enunciating his own theological stance, but he chose to do so without directly attacking Luther. See *ABK*-S, pp. 179–80.

about the call[20] which may be too near some. When have you instructed me? Point out to me one passage in which you have reproved me all your life! In my whole life, you have still never pointed out where I was blameworthy or had erred. You always approach with force. And if you had not wanted to do it with the two of us alone, you should have taken one or two with you.[21]

LUTHER: I did that.

KARLSTADT: If you did that, then may God grant that I am publicly disgraced before all your eyes here.

LUTHER: It will happen.

KARLSTADT: But I know it is not true.

LUTHER: I did it.

KARLSTADT: Who was there?

LUTHER: Philip and Pomeranus.[22]

KARLSTADT: Where?

LUTHER: In your room.

KARLSTADT: That is not true! To be sure you may have been with me, but you have never undertaken to reprove me or to give the articles of the error.

LUTHER: We brought you the note from the university in which the articles which we considered mistaken were specified.

KARLSTADT: Mr. Doctor, at that point you speak arbitrarily. It has still never reached me nor been shown to me. I also remember that the articles of the supposed error were still not stated in writing by the university.

LUTHER: Now dear Mr. Doctor, whenever I say much to you, you make me out to be a liar.

KARLSTADT: If that is true, may God grant that the devils tear

20. Karlstadt probably refers to his book of December 1523, which explained his recent literary silence and developed his view of the inner calling of the minister. See *ABK*-B 2, 81ff. and *ABK*-S, pp. 289–91.

21. This passage and the following bitter recriminations reflecting sharp personal clashes all the way back to 1519 demonstrate that one significant factor in the Luther-Karlstadt quarrel was the lack of personal friendship between the two men.

22. Philip Melanchthon. Is Pomeranus Nicholas Amsdorf? It is often assumed that the incident at issue here is the one mentioned briefly in Melanchthon's letter to Spalatin of April 4, 1524: "Karlstadt is here; today we will meet about his case"; *Corpus Reformatorum*, ed. C. G. Bretschneider (Halis Saxonum: C. A. Schwetschke, 1834ff.), I, 652. But it is possible that Luther refers to an event connected with the suppression of Karlstadt's book against Ochsenfart in the spring of 1522; see *ABK*-B 1, 453ff.; 2, 562–66.

me apart before you all. Indeed you have still never offered it to me.

LUTHER: I brought it to you yourself in your house.

KARLSTADT: Mr. Doctor, what [339] if I had Dr. Jerome's[23] writing in which he charged against me that I would have been given such erroneous articles if I had run after them, how would you stand then? For at that time, the university was still not assembled to draw up the aforesaid articles.[24]

With that, Dr. Luther fell silent awhile and in the silence Dr. Karlstadt turned to the others who sat nearby and said: "Dear brothers, I pray you, don't pay attention to my harsh speech. Such harsh speech is a matter of my complexion but my heart is not on that account wicked or angry." Luther began again and said:

Dear Mr. Doctor, I know you well.

KARLSTADT: I also know you well, indeed more than you yourself imagine.

LUTHER: I know well that you always go about in a grandiose fashion, boast grandly, and want only yourself to be exalted and noticed.

KARLSTADT: If I did that, you should instruct me. But I see clearly who boasts most highly and seeks the greatest honor.

LUTHER: I did reprove you at Leipzig because you were so proud and wanted to dispute before me. Finally I granted you the honor and allowed it to happen.[25]

23. Dr. Hieronymus Schurf, a jurist at Wittenberg.

24. Extant documents do not enable the modern historian to understand this disagreement with any certainty.

25. This is a very one-sided recollection. The first step toward the Leipzig Debate occurred when John Eck attacked Luther's Ninety-five Theses. But Eck's theses and Luther's reply were not printed, and both men decided to let the quarrel drop. If Karlstadt had not published an attack on Eck's theses in May 1518, the Leipzig Debate would never have occurred. The debate was to be between Karlstadt and Eck. When Eck cleverly maneuvered to draw Luther into the debate, there was strong opposition to Luther's involvement by the University of Leipzig and Duke George. In fact Duke George persisted in viewing the debate as one between Karlstadt and Eck, and refused to give Luther a free conduct. Instead, to Luther's great annoyance, Karlstadt's free conduct was extended to include "those whom he might bring with him." When Luther arrived at Leipzig, he strongly opposed Eck's proposals apropos the ground rules for the debate, and they could not reach an agreement for some time. A report was widely circulated that Luther would not debate at all. The Karlstadt-Eck debate began on June 27 but Luther did not even reach agreement on the terms of his involvement until July 4. See Robert H. Fife,

KARLSTADT: Oh, Mr. Doctor, how can you say that? For you know that when I was already disputing you were still uncertain whether or not you would be allowed to dispute. For that, I appeal to Duke George's councilors and the University of Leipzig. But you must always speak in such a way that you maintain your reputation and stir up hatred for other people. According to your regular custom, what else have you accomplished today in your sermon other than to arouse anger and hatred in the first preamble toward the people against whom you intended to preach?

LUTHER: I say what I said before. I preached against the spirits today and will do it again now in spite of anyone who wants to restrain me.

KARLSTADT: Now, dear Mr. Doctor, preach thus and make it good! Other people will also add what they have to say.

LUTHER: Go to it! If you have something, then write about it freely.

KARLSTADT: I will indeed do that without fear.

LUTHER: Nevertheless, you stand among the new prophets.

KARLSTADT: Where they are correct and have the truth; where they are incorrect, the devil stands with them.

LUTHER: Write against me publicly and not secretly.

KARLSTADT: If I knew that you were so eager for that, it would fall to your lot.

LUTHER: Then do it.

KARLSTADT: Agreed!

LUTHER: If you do, I will present you with a gulden for it.

KARLSTADT [340]: A gulden?

LUTHER: If I do not do it, I am a scoundrel.

KARLSTADT: Then give it to me, for I certainly accept the challenge.

Luther then reached in his pocket, pulled out a gold gulden, gave it to Karlstadt, and said:

Take it and attack me boldly now. Attack me sharply!

The Revolt of Martin Luther (New York: Columbia University Press, 1957), pp. 335–52 (esp. 341–43, 350-52); cf. also, *LW* 31, 313-25.

It is quite possible that Luther did want to debate first at Leipzig. Given the circumstances, however, his demand, if it was made, seems quite unjustified. Nevertheless, this kind of personal conflict helps explain the bitterness of the later disagreement between Luther and Karlstadt.

Karlstadt took the gulden, showed it to all bystanders, and said:

Dear brothers, this is a pledge, a sign, that I have authority to write against Dr. Luther. And I beg you all to acknowledge this for me and be my witnesses.

LUTHER: That is not necessary.

Karlstadt bent it, put it in his purse, and gave Dr. Luther his hand on it. And Dr. Luther drank him a toast on it. Karlstadt bid him farewell, and then said:

Mr. Doctor, I beg that you will not prevent me from printing nor otherwise wangle any persecution of me or impediment to my livelihood. For I intend to earn my living with the plow. You shall perceive what the plow will give.

LUTHER: How could I want to prevent you if I want you to write against me? Indeed I gave you the gulden so that you should not spare me. The bolder you attack me, the better I will like it.

The court preacher[26] also said to Karlstadt: "The doctor will not harm your livelihood nor add injury."

Then Karlstadt said to Doctor Luther: "Now it is agreed. If I fail you, it is my loss." And so they shook hands, Karlstadt went home, and Martin preached and afterward traveled to Kahla.[27]

. . . .

26. Wolfgang Stein, preacher at the castle at Weimar, was traveling with Luther.

27. A final paragraph lists some of the persons who were present at the parley.

4

Gradualism Exposed: Karlstadt's *Whether One Should Proceed Slowly*

In late September 1524, the princes banished Karlstadt from electoral Saxony, forcing him to leave behind his small child and pregnant wife at Orlamünde. Even before he left, however, he responded to Luther's challenge to literary warfare by sending his brother-in-law, Gerhard Westerburg, to Switzerland with eight tracts for publication. One of these, *Whether One Should Proceed Slowly* (published at Basel in mid-November 1524), was his belated reply to Luther's Eight Sermons of March 1522. Whereas Luther had called for tactical delay for the sake of the weaker neighbor who had not yet been persuaded by preaching and the princes who favored cautious progress, Karlstadt issued the radical demand that every local congregation must implement changes immediately without regard to those who might be offended. The radical's perennial impatience with caution, compromise, and tactical delay is vividly expressed here by Karlstadt. Gordon Rupp has suggested that this book is "perhaps his best polemical writing" (*Patterns of Reformation* [Philadelphia: Fortress, 1969], p. 139).

For a discussion of the contents, see below (pp. 154–57) and Ulrich Bubenheimer, "Scandalum et ius divinum," *Zeitschrift der Savigny-Stiftung für Rechtsgeschichte* (1973), pp. 322–24.

The German text is in Hertzsch 1, 73–97. A modern German text is in Heinhold Fast, ed., *Der linke Flügel der Reformation* (Bremen: Carl Schünemann, 1962), pp. 249ff.

Whether One Should Proceed Slowly and Avoid Offending the Weak in Matters that Concern God's Will

Andreas Karlstadt

1524

To [74] my especially beloved brother in Christ, Bartel Bach,[1] town clerk in Joachimsthal, I, Andreas Karlstadt, wish the knowledge of God through Jesus Christ our Lord.

Upon my report, dear brother, of some changes which occurred here, you wrote to me that for yourself you would like to move slowly hereafter, and through such writing secretly led me to understand that one should proceed slowly rather than quickly or suddenly in order to avoid offending the weak. You do nothing other than what the whole world now does which shouts: "Weak, weak, sick, sick, not too fast, slowly, slowly." Therefore I do not blame you. Since, however, in this case you say, "slow, sick," with the great crowd, albeit more courteously and considerately, I must therefore tell you that neither in this case nor in other matters concerning God should you consider how the great crowd speaks or judges, but rather look only at God's Word. For at the least it is clear that the princes of the biblical scholars and the whole crowd formerly have erred and can err. For that reason, God ordained what the princes and also the whole crowd or council should sacrifice for their ignorance or error (Lev. 4 [:1ff.]). By that command God clearly pointed out for all time that all learned persons, princes, and the whole crowd can err and stumble. Accordingly, God has also sent word in general and in particular that each person [75] should hurry to righteousness for himself and that no one is to follow the crowd, and thereby retreat from the right (Exod. 23 [:2]).

1. An influential person with whom Karlstadt had had friendly relations for several years. Karlstadt hoped (in vain) that Bach might support him instead of Luther. See Hertzsch 1, 102 and *ABK*-B 1, 202–3, 415; 2, 179.

God also calls it harlotry and adulterous eyes when one considers things other than his rule of conduct, that is, God's Word. God has forbidden us to follow our own thoughts. All our good intentions to act or speak the way other people act or speak or the way it seems good to us are completely cut off and amputated. The wisdom of all wise persons must fall to the ground and perish if divine wisdom is to arise (Luke 15 [:1–2]; Isa. [29:14]; Matt. 16 [:4, 13ff.]; Deut. 12 [:8]). It is not only your own wisdom, dear brother, which must become nothing and foolishness, but also the wisdom of all other men so that you allow neither learned nor unlearned to move you and so that you concern yourself directly with the naked truth which makes you free and does not allow you to be ashamed even to eternity.

Notice here that just as you yourself are a reed which you should shun, so too all learned persons should be a weak reed to you [Matt. 11:7]. The naked truth alone should be your foundation and rock. If you had that, then you would remain unconcerned and unvacillating even though all learned persons changed and the apostles fell away, if that were possible. For Paul says: "If I or an angel taught otherwise, he should be accursed" (Gal. 1 [:8]). He who understands and grasps the truth fundamentally remains in it even though Paul preaches against it. Therefore everyone who wants to stand firm before the wind and the waves should be zealous to learn the true grounds of God. That is the reason why God, through Moses, commanded all Jews to hang tassels, small flaps, and yellow cords from their garments so they would remember to think of God's commands as often as they became aware of these small flaps which they had to look at daily (Num. 15 [:37ff.]).

It follows from this that we are fastened to Scripture, that no one may judge according to the good pleasure of his heart (Jer. 23 [:16ff.]), and also that those who look to things other than God's Word promote harlotry. And truly, it is genuine harlotry and spiritual adultery, however small or little such gazing about and craving may seem to the flesh and reason. For God, who is a husband of the created spirit, is scorned, or neglected and forgotten as soon as the soul considers things other than his Word in divine matters—if it [76] must always be the case that no one can serve two lords, that a servant of two lords must leave one when he clings to the other. Now spiritual adultery is always a devilish, outrageous blasphemy. All men who consider the princes of the highly learned or a great crowd such as a council more than God's Word, or who also consider something other than God's true sayings fall into this blasphemy.

Therefore, dear brother, you, no less than the most lowly, are bound instantly, immediately, earnestly, and industriously to look to God's judgments which are correct and true in themselves; you are not to notice the strong or weak. The great crowd can err and make one err. Sometimes the anointed[2] also write of their anointing. For they are externally smeared and also fall into error which displeases God. Because that is the way things are now, see to it that you come to understand divine righteousness and truth and instantly pay attention to God's sayings. And see to it that all learned ones in Scripture are nothing to you, and that no one waits until the other person follows.

In Acting One Should Also Not Consider Others

Now as I have just demonstrated through scriptural evidence that no one should look around at the other person or wait until the others follow when it concerns knowledge of the truth (John 5 [:39–41]), so too when it concerns performance, we should do all God's commands according to our ability and should not wait until the foolish or weak follow. For God has always commanded that we all should learn his covenant and act accordingly. It always stands written: Teach it and keep it so that you act according to it (Deut. 4 [:2]; 5 [:1]). To do it is prescribed to all of us, and each one should do what God commands even though the whole world holds back and does not want to follow.

See here! I ask you whether a son should not honor his parents until the weak follow along and also understand and want to honor their parents? You would always have to reply: "Certainly those who understand should not rob parents of their honor nor wait until all minors develop understanding and will." I ask whether one should not stop coveting other people's goods until [77] the others follow? May one steal until the thieves stop stealing? Likewise I ask you in the case of all the commands whether it is fitting that we wait until the others have learned them and want to

2. The ordained priests and bishops.

follow them and do what God desires? Now just as I asked that about the commands which concern love of neighbor, so too I ask that about the works and deeds which concern God's honor directly.

To be specific, I ask whether I should leave idols[3] standing which God commands me to take away until all the weak follow in their removal? I ask further whether I may blaspheme God as long as the others do not cease blaspheming? If you say yes, then the enemies of Christ and God may also rightly say that the murderers may murder, the thieves steal, adulterers commit adultery, and similar rascals engage in all kinds of vice until all rascals become pious. For there is one intention and one ground in all commands. I will never say that the rascals may sin for I know that even those who fall or break God's command out of ignorance sin and must suffer their punishment for it (Lev. 5 [:17]). How much more those who take the part of the adulterers, thieves, murderers, and blasphemers (Ps. 50 [:16ff.])! They shall always be punished along with those who do such things for themselves. The Lord says: The servant who knows the will of his master and acts otherwise shall be beaten with many stripes (Luke 12 [:47]). God will beat him who sins out of ignorance. How much more forcibly and vigorously, however, will God punish the one who sins against his command to please a rascal! Paul says: You shall have no fellowship with the servants of idols, adulterers, and the like [II Cor. 6:14ff.]. And you think one must act slowly and forsake evil gradually! But I know that St. Peter will also gradually turn the key to heaven which he is to have and will get it stuck in the lock, or turn it the wrong way; and he will always unlock for them as slowly as they have come.

What should I say? Should we teach God's commands slowly? Should we wait for the crowd? Should one look at the others and wait to see who wants to be first? Indeed, how well would it please the great princes if the people would come as willingly for tithes, rents, and compulsory service as they come for divine services? They throw the disobedient [78] into the towers and stocks and leave them in the stocks until their subjects become obedient; and through their fury they declare against themselves the judgment

3. Karlstadt believed that the common people esteemed images in an idolatrous way (see above, p. 25, n. 7).

which God will display toward them and which they display toward the disobedience of others. What lord can tolerate it if he commands his servants to do something and then they all stand around and no one wants to be first or begin first?

God will punish them all together when he summons those who failed to appear even though they adduce golden excuses and trot out the best reasons of brotherly love. For there should always be a great and special love between married people. Nevertheless, Christ says that he who excused himself because of his wife [Luke 14:20] was unworthy of his meal. Each person (who understands correctly) should act correctly without timidity and without gazing about.

When one says, "You should be indulgent for the sake of brotherly love," it means nothing at all because it is not yet decided whether their brotherly love is not an anti-Christian cloak which is by all means as wicked and destructive as any invention of the pope. But I will not examine that now. But I say that Christ has abolished and cut off all brotherly love if it stands against his command or turns one from God even a very little. For love fulfills God's commands, and it is impossible to love Christ and act contrary to his command or not do what Christ commands. That follows from this saying: If you love me, then keep my command (John 14 [:21]). "He who is not with me is against me" (Matt. 12 [:30]). He who does not hate father and mother, wife and children cannot be my disciple, etc. [Luke 14:26]. Now since it is the case that it is impossible to love Christ and not live according to his commands or to stand still and look at another and wait to see whether the other person will or will not do what pleases God, they therefore will not tie an apron or curtain over my eyes so that I forsake something which God wants or do something which God forbids even though they preached and wrote to me about offenses and brotherly love for a thousand years.[4]

The truth says: "He who put his hand to the plow and looks back is not fit for the kingdom of God" (Luke 9 [:62]). Christ said that of the one whom he called to follow him. And that person answered thus: Lord, I will follow you, but permit me to bless or say farewell to my family. Now if that person [79] who

4. See below, p. 111, for what is probably Luther's response.

looks out for others to whom he otherwise might well bid farewell is not fit for the kingdom of God, how fit will those be who overlook God's commands and hold back for the sake of others who do not want to begin? Lot's wife looked back and became a pillar of salt (Gen. 19 [:26]). What may become of those who look back on the sluggish and lazy brethren who sometimes purposely remain blind and lazy?

When Christ said to Peter, "Follow me," and Peter said, "But what should this one do?" Christ answered: 'If I want him to remain until I come again, what does that matter to you?" (John 21 [:19ff]). Notice there that even if God allows it to happen that some are lazy or unwilling to learn and act properly, and you understand that—has he not called you sufficiently? Will you ask what the others should do or when they will come? No! "Follow" is what he commands. Do not stand still and ponder whether the others also follow.

Did Peter ask those Christians who were vexed that he had baptized the heathen Cornelius about brotherly love (Acts 9–11)? He did what he understood was God's will and did not ask anyone. But when his brethren accosted him because of his act, he gave an answer which God wanted. Nevertheless, there was in Peter's act something which one might have been able to forbid or censure because of Christ's statement: You shall not go into the way of the heathen [Matt. 10:5]. Because of that, Peter should rightly have considered the offense. But Peter was not concerned about the offense. What shall we do in those matters which God commands or forbids with explicit statements? Shall we avoid the offense? Now if someone says, "Christ, not Peter, is an example for us; therefore give me an example from Christ," I respond: Christ spoke with a Samaritan woman, and the Jews were not accustomed to speak with Samaritans, and his disciples were also astonished by it (John 4). But Christ was not concerned about offending them, but rather did freely what his father wanted. In the following I will illustrate that with other examples such as the sabbath, the temple, sacrifice, fasting, prayer, and the like.

They adduce Paul so vigorously in the matter of offenses and in things of that sort because they want to force and compel one to conclude that one should go slowly in things which pertain to God. All day they shout: "The weak, the weak," etc. However I well know how to subdue them and may say freely that Paul [80] did not act slowly in items that were greater than ours were here. Nor did he consider the fact that some took offense or were sick, unwise, and weak. We read that many thousands of Jews had become believers (Acts 21 [:20ff.]). They were greatly annoyed that Paul taught and preached a departure from Moses, namely, that one should not circumcise children or live according to tradition, etc. There you observe that Paul was not concerned about offending so many thousands of unwise Jews, but rather preached freely and did not spare the weak. Here you will answer: "It seems to me that preaching and acting are two different things." To this I say that preaching is an action like any other action: it is not to be done for nothing, etc. Moreover, Paul prevented circumcision with acts. How then can one say that we should be Paulinists and not begin to act upon anything which tends against brotherly love? That Paul subsequently did something by which he quelled the outcry against him [Acts 21:23ff.] does not force me to say that Paul therefore did not prevent circumcision with deeds, for his Epistle to the Galatians is too clear for anyone to conceal it. And from the same epistle, one must conclude that Paul was not concerned about the weak, but rather drew them from Moses with prompt words when he said: "You foolish persons, do you allow yourselves to be circumcised" [Gal. 3:1ff.]?

So you have a candid justification for my view that we here[5] were not obliged to refrain either in teaching or activity from carrying out God's commands until our neighbors and the guzzlers at Wittenberg followed.

Each Congregation, However Little or Great It May Be, Should See for Itself that It Acts Properly and Well and Waits for No One

God has given a general law to which the whole believing people, and each congregation and each person should hold and conform. The same law, which God also calls covenant, was rightly recited or read to the whole people. This was read not so

5. Karlstadt undoubtedly wrote the book while at Orlamünde. For a discussion of Karlstadt's activity and theology during this period, see *ABK*-S, chaps. 6–7.

that the whole crowd or corporate body would be the kind of dead body which the blind jurists invent when they speak of a corporate body and say that the same body can neither hear nor see nor do anything.[6] Rather this was read so that [81] the people would have ears ready to hear, eyes ready to see, and limbs ready to do all righteousness which pleases God (Deut. 29 [:4ff.]). Accordingly God also complained about the lazy persons and threatened to punish such negligent ones who had ears and still did not hear, eyes and did not see, limbs and did not work. It is certainly true that Moses summoned the whole multitude of the Jews together and related God's commands to the whole Jewish crowd. But he always said that they should do what he taught them,[7] and that they should be satisfied both with his teaching and also with the deeds so that they would not add anything to or take anything away from the teaching (Deut. 12 [:29–32]), and likewise that they would not plan to do any work for the service of God other than what he taught them to do. Lev. 16 [:1ff.]). Thus Moses bound his people so firmly to God's doctrine, practices, laws, and to the work of the law that they could neither teach nor do otherwise than as they had heard. And because of the bond, Moses called the law a covenant, although there were also other reasons.

That God's covenant concerns every individual community and in addition each household so that no community or household may stand still until other places become intelligent and active is shown so often in Deuteronomy alone that I think it unnecessary to adduce evidence. So often it stands written: You should maintain the laws and practices of God in your gates (Deut. 17 [:8–13?]). You should choose and establish judges who are to punish those who break the covenant (Deut. 26 [cf. 16:18]). Has God spoken this word only to the crowd or corporate body as a whole: The Lord your God commands you to act according to all this law, and all these practices and laws from your whole heart and soul as you have promised to your Lord (Deut. 5 [:27ff.])? Who may say that one must keep God's commands only in some

6. Karlstadt had a doctorate in canon and Roman law, but he rejected canon law when he adopted *sola scriptura*. For the continuing influence of his legal studies, see above, p. 7, n. 1.

7. Karlstadt here has marginal references to Deut. 4 [:1ff.]; 5 [:1]; 6 [:1-9]; 8 :[1, 11]; 11 [:1, 8, 18ff.].

places? And that we may break God's commands in other places? If you say that God commanded the Jews to erect stones only in some places, I will also say that God ordered and commanded that we should write his covenant[8] not only in some places, but rather on the doorposts of the houses as a reminder (Deut. 6 [:5–9]), and also on the gates so that they are suspended and stand before the eyes of the household servants and each community and that thereby they should be reminded to keep God's commands[9]—not only some commands, but [82] all commands; not only the Jews who heard Moses at that very time, but also their descendants (for Moses says, "Your children and children's children" [Deut. 4:9]); not one day but every day ("All your life," Moses says). Each community should have its Levite who proclaims the covenant of peace and truth to them. And the father of each household should inculcate, repeat, and relate God's word to his children. From this it certainly follows that each community and household should see to it that they understand God's commands and do them. God is so far from wanting us to wait until others follow and become pious that he has commanded that one should punish the godless just as one punishes other vices. And in addition, he has commanded that one should destroy and demolish whole cities which wanted to remain in their idolatry or did not want to walk in the right path (Deut. 13 [:1–19]; 17 [:2–7]). Our scripturally learned persons and our princes amaze me greatly because they punish fleshly adultery and allow spiritual adultery to remain unpunished. The spiritual they want to cast down with their breath and wind, and the fleshly they want to control with swords, iron, fire, and the executioner's wheels. But is that not deplorable behavior among Christians? Is it not a devilish thing that they are more concerned about and punish more roughly those who dishonor men than those who dishonor God? Moses commands one to destroy the idolatrous or spiritual adulterers no less than the fleshly adulterers (Deut. 13 [:1–19]; 17 [:2–7]). If they read their Paul properly, they would certainly find that Paul punished those who served idols no less than those who visited harlots. Nor does it have to be correct just because they want to have it thus and want to defend their honor and their beautiful image.

8. In the margin: "Covenant of his ten words."
9. There are marginal references to Deut. 26 [:16]; 27 [:1–3]; 28 [:1, 14].

Action Should Immediately and Always Follow Understanding

A gracious God has produced some external works and thereby shown his fatherly love. One of these works is that God has given divine wisdom and understanding (Deut. 4 [:3–6]) to our patriarchs in miraculous visions and stories through his lofty, noble word and to us through our ancestors.[10] Therefore all people should rightly say: Surely this is an excellent people which has such high knowledge and righteous customs [83] and laws [cf. v. 6]? And God has placed his covenant, which contains our wisdom and understanding, before us so that in all our activity, both active and passive, we work, live, and order things intelligently and wisely (Deut. 29 [:9]). For in all things God wants to have intelligent servants who know what they do or suffer, why they do or suffer it, and for whose honor. What God sends and why he sends it should be understood in sweet and sour, in an active and a passive manner. As Moses says: Keep now the word of this covenant and act according to it so that you are intelligent in all that you do (Deut. 29 [:9]). And Paul: See that you walk prudently, not as the unwise, but as the wise; therefore do not be ignorant but rather understand whatever the will of the Lord is (Eph. 5 [:15–17]). Through Isaiah, therefore, God deplores the fact that they do not consider his work (Isa. 5 [:1–7]). And Christ often censured his apostles because they did not understand his work or teaching. But they, that is, understanding and wisdom, should be possessed not only when you do something, but also when you suffer something, so that you know what, why, for whose honor and for whose benefit you suffer. For that is the peculiarity of suffering. As Isaiah says: Trouble or mockery gives understanding (Isa. 28 [:11–12?]). And Moses: God assails you so that you are ashamed of your sins (Lev. 26 [:40ff.]). And Paul: Affliction gives birth to patience; patience, however, brings knowledge or experience (Rom. 5 [:3–5]). For that experience is knowledge and the complete work of which James writes (Jas. 1 [:4–5]). Without knowledge, no work of God is complete. Without knowledge we are like a tongue and horse in which there is no understanding [Jas. 3:3ff.]. Accordingly, God's Word is revealed to us out of great grace so that we thereby become

10. See *ABK-S*, pp. 263–64 for a discussion of this passage.

intelligent, wise, understanding, that is, through self-renunciation.[11] It is, however, a great and highly esteemed thing that God's secret is revealed to us. The worldly-wise consider it a great treasure when one is a councilor of a mortal prince. And everyone holds before his eyes a person who is beloved by the prince. How much more highly is that one to be esteemed and how highly and dearly should that one to whom God has revealed his secret regard himself, especially since he has a new, divine, and superhuman wisdom? That is the first reason God has revealed and disclosed his secret to us.

The [84] second is that we should have an eternal and immovable remembrance of all his words and stories so that all our life and at all times nothing slips our memory in order that we always fear God and cling to him. The remembrance, however, should be passionate, industrious, and powerful. It does not stand still, but rather breaks forth with ardor and is active. For it is a common rule: "Cursed is he who does or performs the work of the Lord sluggishly" (Jer. 48 [:10]) or performs it deceptively. Although the passage speaks of the vengeance of God when it says, "Cursed is he who keeps back his sword from blood" (Jer. 48 [:10]), nevertheless it is much more true in other activities. For if it is true that God, who is merciful to forgive, wants to have prompt punishment, how much more accursed and abominable before God is he who is lazy in bursting forth with works for the betterment of his neighbor. God wants a completely willing giver, one who gives quickly and voluntarily. A ready, willing mind inclined to action pleases God (II Cor. 9 [:7]). All this flows from the perpetual and fervent remembrance of divine words. He who remembers divine teaching properly and well cannot stand still or be idle or peevish when God's sayings obligate and impel him to action. If he holds still in a situation where he can and should work, that is a certain sign that he has forgotten or does not have the kind of remembrance that he should have—that is, from his whole heart (Deut. 29).

Concerning that, someone may raise a question: You want a servant of God to be bound to act at all times (Deut. 11 [:1]). There is, indeed, a basis for that since it stands written: You shall

11. *Gelassenheit*—an extremely important word in Karlstadt's theology. See *ABK*-S, 180ff., 216ff. Below, p. 115, Luther denounces Karlstadt's use of mystical terminology.

act or work according to divine law all the time or all your life (Tob. 4 [:20]). You should always praise God. I will praise God all the time (Ps. 34 [:1]). He who is a friend always loves his friend (Prov. 17 [:17])—that is, a friend always shows his love externally in the way Christ said: "By this they will know that you are my disciples if you love one another" (John 13 [:35]). On the other hand, however, I also see that it is written: Each activity has its time (Eccles. 9 [3:1ff.]). That is, no activity may continue perpetually. For a time, it is done; then it ceases. Also God has so established some commands that we must keep them at particular times and not for our whole life or every day as the Hebrew sense and you allege. For instance, God has established the sabbath on the seventh day, the seventh week, the seventh year, the fiftieth year (which also came from the number seven), the Passover feast [85] at one time in the year, the feast of booths, and the like at a particular time. These must occur only at one time and not every day.

Here is my answer. If such figurative sayings bound us according to the letter just as they bound the Jews at one time,[12] God's words—that is: You should keep God's commands every day (Deut. 11 [:13])—would still be true. For these words "every day" mean that each person should keep God's command according to the time, place, and condition God commanded. There is a time when we should awake and be industrious. There is a time to sleep. If there are poor, we should help. If we have no needy persons, our hands may rest. Nonetheless, we must do or act every day according to God's commands; we must celebrate every seventh day, etc., always come to the help of the poor, destitute, imprisoned, naked, etc., [and] forgive a debt to the impoverished if we have such debtors. If we have none, then God's law does not bind us just as the poor were not bound to expensive sacrifices in the way the rich were. This, however, stands fast: You should complete God's command every day. You should actively demonstrate toward your neighbor your love for God and neighbor every day.

It is also the same with the removal of the God-blaspheming and Christ-blaspheming images or masses. Where we, who con-

12. But Karlstadt does not believe they do. Christians should apply these statements to themselves in a figurative, not a literal way. For a discussion of Karlstadt's view of figurative exegesis, see *ABK*-S, pp. 112ff., 265ff.

fess God, rule and find idols, we should remove them and behave toward them as God commanded. We should also do that for our whole life or every day. Yes, in the same way, when we find them in our community, each community, that is, every community in its city, is responsible to restrain the error.[13] This must always be right and stand the test well: You should act according to God's commands every day. That is right and good when it is properly understood.

The figurative commands imprison and ensnare only the weak.[14] And because of the weak it is good that the figurative commands have been kept and still should be. As Paul says: All things are legitimate, but all things do not edify (I Cor. 11 [10:23]). Also: Although you have correct knowledge or understanding, it is still not complete. Nor do you know as you should (I Cor. 8 [:2]). Because the understanding of many Jews was small and their blindness great, they were not free but rather imprisoned and obligated to keep God's figurative statements although God's intention was different from the sound of his words. And the weak lacked God's eternal will. Therefore [86] they had to keep the sabbath and other holidays and fleshly, righteous practices such as bathing in water, etc., according to the sound of God's words and according to God's veiled will until they understood God's true righteousness and righteous truth more fundamentally. However, he who broke or transgressed one of these figurative commands of God had to give an honest justification as Christ did and David when he did not give God any external sacrifice (Ps. 39 [40:6–9]). That issue does not belong here, but I have mentioned it so that one would know in what manner the divine commands must be kept.

Figuratively, "every day" signifies at the proper and designated time; fundamentally, however, one must keep God's commands every day insofar as the instance demands. There are some commands which require a particular time, place, or occasion. One must keep these commands every day, that is, whenever there is an opportunity. And no one may look around at another who became lazy and deserved punishment. Some commands imply no particular occasion, time, or place. One must follow these commands

13. The marginal reference to Deut. 14, 15 is unclear.
14. See n. 12 above.

perpetually and never depart from them or act contrary to them. These commands are in the latter category: You shall not make, have, or tolerate images; you shall not steal, murder, commit adultery, bear false witness, covet another's goods, etc. Such commands bind us at all times and in all places. He who acts contrary to one of these any place whatsoever is a transgressing, disobedient, unrighteous despiser of God. Nor should he look around at any crowd or council for he already has his command against which he should not act. Therefore he should not make any image or tolerate those that have been made in the places where they rule, whether they represent God, Christ, or the saints. Nor should he blaspheme God or do anything of the sort forbidden by God's covenant (which Moses expounds—and the prophets further unfold Moses' deposition) unless he has received a certain and nondeceptive command from God to act contrary to a command—as Moses received a command from God to make the bird statues over the mercy-seat, to make twelve oxen to hold the sea, and to erect a snake in the wilderness.[15]

He who has no such command from God knows that he sins and disobeys God's voice which has commanded that we should not make any image or tolerate those already made in those places [87] where the alleged believers rule. In the same way, too, no one should steal, murder, commit adultery, or covet another's goods. If he acts contrary to one of these, he is disobedient, unrighteous, and sinful. Nor will he justify himself by any crowd of weak or sick people. However, if God would command someone to steal, rob, murder, commit adultery, or covet another's goods, and he would be certain of God's intention, he should steal as the children of Israel stole from the Egyptians (Exod. 12 [:35–36]), [and] murder as Moses murdered the kings of Sihon and Heshbon, etc.[16] Without God's command, however, we must do all that God has included in his ten words and have regard for no one except God's command and ourselves (so that we do or forsake what truly pleases God).

God always speaks according to the capacity of the Hebrew

15. Karlstadt is replying to Luther's Third Sermon of March 11, 1522 (see above, pp. 25–27).

16. Karlstadt refers to Acts 7 [:24], Deut. 2 [:26–36], and Deut. 29 [:6–7] which speaks of Sihon, king of Heshbon.

tongue. Some, however, resist God's prohibition and Word with this proviso, "Not every day." Because of the weak, they say, one should delay and not proceed at all. But is that not the same as if they said that we should allow the council to determine beforehand what we should do and to what degree we should serve God? That is certainly the same thing as this statement: For the sake of the weak, one should not fulfill God's command quickly, but rather tarry until they become intelligent and strong. Nevertheless, that could be the case if it were stated properly as Paul has taught. But it is strange that with delay and disregard for clear divine commands they want to raise up the weak whom they really push further down with their horns and shoulders, as Ezekiel prophesied of the horns of oxen [cf. Ezek. 34:21]. They have no teaching for that at all. Likewise, Paul, whom they inappropriately and nonsensically adduce as a model for sparing the weak, is entirely opposed to them. What should I say? I say that this outcry, "Not too fast, not too soon, spare, spare, the weak, the weak, the sick, the sick" is an open addition to God's Word. It is contrary to the Scripture: You should not add (Deut. 4 [:2]). This postponement (I restrain myself, I spare and delay until the weak come) is also a discontinuance of divine works. It is contrary to the Scripture: You should neither add nor subtract [Deut. 4:2]. And contrary to: You should do exactly as God commanded you and always act thus (Deut. 11 [:8, 18ff.]).

Offense [88] and Love of Neighbor Are a Devilish Cloak for All Kinds of Evil

It is not right to adduce offense [of the weak] and brotherly love and to honor idols under the pretext of offense and brotherly love and to allow the mass and other blasphemies of God to sprout and bloom. In a little book that I am writing about offense,[17] I will announce how one is to evaluate and understand that. At this point, however, I want to say that our images are placed or erected to ruin, trap, and destroy man as God has said through Moses and his prophets. In addition, the idols are more dangerous in Christendom than fleshly houses of prostitution and more conducive to spiritual adultery than any harlot or rascal. Therefore those who,

17. This book was never published.

under the cloak and pretext of brotherly love, command us to keep the idols (which the laity call saints) in the churches, on the hills, in the valleys, and at the crossroads until the weak become strong do not demonstrate a genuine brotherly love. For they preach brotherly injury and not brotherly service or love. Such pretense is nothing other than a rogue's cloak and a concealed snare for the destruction of poor souls, if God really speaks truly and if Paul—who teaches the opposite in the case of offending [the weak]—speaks correctly.

We should take such horrible things from the weak, and snatch them from their hands and not consider whether they cry, scream, or curse because of it. The time will come when they who now curse and damn us will thank us. By a comparison, I will show you that he who would forcibly break the will of fools would manifest toward them the brotherly love which is genuine and best. Of the fools who keep idols, Isaiah says that they do not understand their foolishness nor know that they keep a destructive, foolish thing [Isa. 44:1ff., 18]. I want that to be my first example. Therefore, I ask whether, if I should see that a little innocent child holds a sharp pointed knife in his hand and wants to keep it, I would show him brotherly love if I would allow him to keep the dreadful knife as he desires with the result that he would wound or kill himself, or when I would break his will and take the knife? You must always say that if you take from the child what brings injury to him [89], you do a fatherly or brotherly Christian deed. For Christ has depicted for us genuinely Christian and brotherly love in the passages where he says: "If your hand offends you, cut it off and throw it from you" (Matt. 18 [:8]). Christ said that in order to point to genuine brotherly love. And Paul agrees with Christ when he speaks of offenses.

If it is the case that I am responsible and each person is obliged, if he loves God and his neighbor, to take from the foolish their dreadful and offensive things irrespective of the fact that they therefore become angry, howl, and curse, why do they say so much about brotherly love, asserting that for the sake of brotherly love, we should allow idols and other offenses to stand or remain until the weak follow? What they call brotherly love is really brotherly injury and offense. Their love is like the love of a foolish mother who allows her children to keep their willfulness and thus permits them to go to the hangman. Christ in no way said that we should proceed slowly in the case of offenses when we want to remove them and cast them away from us. He says: Cut off, cut down, cast away from yourself so that you are not offended. Moses also says: Your eye should not spare him, and you should not pity him or conceal him, but rather kill him; your hand should be the first against him (Deut. 13 [:8-9]; 33 [:9]; Mic. 7 [:10]). Moses says that about men who cause offense. How much more does this saying urge the removal of offenses (through which ignorant souls fall) which have neither flesh nor spirit, neither blood nor breath, and for whose improvement no one may hope. Moses certainly wants to say and cry out: Spare not! Destroy them! Your hand should be the first!

Now he who wants to add to these words and say that one should go slowly, not quickly, and should spare the weak and not begin suddenly censures the word of Christ and Moses and adds his own against God and makes himself a false Christ and prophet. Christ says: If your eye offends you, that is, if you understand that your eye offends you, tear it out and cast it from you. When does he say, "Go slowly, do not be hasty," or "Spare the weak?" O great and dreadful blindness! If the world knew what injury came to simple souls [90] from idols and other offenses, they would take a bite out of their fingers before they allowed such fraud. Is it not a rogue's cloak when they preach and command hellish, brotherly injury under the form of brotherly love? O devourers of the world! Christ says: It is better for you to cut it off, tear it out, and cast it from you than for you to be thrown into hellfire with the offending things (Matt. 18 [:8]). I have written about all aspects of the injuries which come from the retention of the devilish saints (which our neighbors call saints and we call idols) against the miserable and wretched goat Emser, but it was suppressed because of the new papists.[18] Those, however, who now read and understand the Bible notice well how violently and contrary to God they have treated me.

18. The Catholic Hieronymus Emser wrote a sharp attack on Karlstadt's *Von Abtuhung der Bilder* in April 1522. Karlstadt responded, but the university had just censored and suppressed Karlstadt's work against the Catholic Ochsenfart (and indirectly Luther) in April. Hence it was not possible for Karlstadt to publish this work against Emser. See *ABK*-B 1, 394ff., 453–59 and *ABK*-S, pp. 174–75.

The devil has invented this rogue's cloak just as he also devised the saying that images are the laity's books.[19] For the devil has thereby thievishly stolen the honor of God's Word and given it to the dreadful, miserable creatures which blaspheme God, and has compared God's Word to the idolatrous mudholes which God hates and wants us to hate and flee. That is not to say how God is disgraced through idols and the weak person is destroyed. Would that a patron of idols would step forward and tell me how the servants of idols have a root which produces gall and bitterness (Deut. 29 [:16ff., esp. v. 18]; Exod. 23 [:24]). If they knew that, they would spit upon themselves (that is said as an aside): "Shame! You destroyers of the Scriptures and snatchers of souls." If as little danger and as trifling injury arose from idols as you allege, God would not have forbidden them so often through Moses and the prophets. Nor would he have said: You will destroy yourselves if you make images or any kind of form, etc. (Deut. 4 [15ff.]). Papist sophist, God speaks of our destruction. Contrary to God, however, they speak of an act of brotherly love. Notice there how they understand Paul who says that the weak, that is, the unwise, perish because of food offered to idols (I Cor. 8 [:10–11]).

It does not follow that because God commanded the Jews not to exterminate the heathen (their enemies) hurriedly or quickly, but rather by degrees in a leisurely or gradual manner, therefore Christians should also proceed gradually and slowly when they abolish offenses. . . .

Now [91] I will anticipate the enemies of divine righteousness and show them what they could say if they opened their eyes. And then I shall immediately knock down their argument. I ask thus: Do not the servants of idols and the protectors of images have a good argument for protecting and keeping their idols from the fire for a long time even though they will not defend them eternally? For God speaks as follows: "I will not drive them out in one year lest the land become waste and wild animals multiply against you. Gradually or with leisure, over a period of time I will drive them out before you until you increase and possess the land" (Exod. 23 [:29–30]). God said that of the heathen whose land the Jews were to occupy. And he said, "I will not drive them

19. A common medieval view since Pope Gregory the Great (590–604).

out in one year. Gradually and slowly I will expel them." That, however, is fitting and appropriate to the question of the removal of images, especially as a comparison. For if the Jews were to exterminate their enemies who might do a great injury gradually or over a period of time, how much more should they gradually eliminate the idols which could inflict no injury on them. . . .

My answer [92]. O you miserable blindness, you imprudent evil! With what strange patches you mend your cloak! You cannot help yourself with cunning in that way. We would certainly want to oppose you for the sake of the truth, even if you had better founded reasons to push your handicraft longer and to make your countenance more praiseworthy. For the Scriptures you cited clink just as if the abbot in Pegau, who can also produce a counterfeit argument, had sung them.

Now let us see how this text supports you. It is true, as these patrons of idols insist, that God did not want to drive out the heathen in one year and that God forbade the Jews to proceed hurriedly, quickly, and suddenly. However, when you say that one should therefore also proceed gradually and leisurely with the removal of the idols, that is your little invention. (I do not speak to you, dear brother,[20] but to a patron of idols.) It is your wisdom and your addition and not God's addition when you say, "For the sake of the weak." I ask where it stands written that the Jews should expel their enemies slowly for the sake of the weak? God has given his reason. If God is sufficiently intelligent and faithful, then his reason is also good, honest, and sufficient. But God does not say, "You shall act gradually and proceed slowly for the sake of the weak." Indeed, for the sake of the weak, God would have destroyed all heathen at once. God forbade the Jews to have friendship and fellowship with the heathen so that the Jews would not fall away from him and so that the heathen would not be a trap and snare to them and cause their downfall. God has given a reason by which one should stand more zealously than by a battlement and not censure God's reason through human addition. God says: You shall not destroy them quickly and suddenly lest the land become waste and the wild animals multiply against you (Exod. 23 [:29]). There you see the reason which is divine, honest, and

20. Bartel Bach (see n. 1 above).

sufficient and which Moses also related at another place without further addition (Deut. 7 [:22]).

. . . .

These [95] narratives[21] show clearly that the Jews were neither to make alliances with the heathen nor to proceed slowly in destroying the altars. They also show that God prosecuted and punished them because they were too sluggish. Now since God is intelligent enough and adds to his words when and where one should proceed gradually and slowly rather than quickly or suddenly, it is certainly a great anti-Christian outrage to censure God's wisdom and add something to his words, especially when the addition is contrary to God's will and results in injury to the neighbor's soul. It is an outrage to say that at these points one should wait for the sake of the weak and go slowly when God has not said that we should go slowly or gradually—especially when through delay one brings the weak further from the way of truth and into greater error. It is written, "Cursed be he who makes a blind person stray from the way" (Deut. 27 [:18]). How much more is he accursed who makes the blind soul err in God's way or Word? Each person, however, who allows an offense, a mousetrap, or the devil's bait to stand in his brother's way does that. But blessed is he who tears away his brother's destruction even against his will and grieves him to whom he wishes happiness so that he does him good, as a father angers his child whom he loves when he takes a sharp knife from him and angers him.

In the case of offenses against the faith, he who has a strong spirit and can suffer somewhat may tear out, throw down, and break in pieces before he preaches as did Gideon although he was afraid and smashed the altar of Baal at night (Judg. 6 [:25–27]). Yes indeed, I say that it is unnecessary that one attack public offenses with preaching before the act follows. The action of Gideon shows that, as does that of Asa who purged the abominations of the idols and deposed his mother [I Kings 15:9ff.], Jehoshaphat [II Chron. 17:6ff.], Jehu [II Kings 10:18ff.], Hezekiah [II Chron. 29:1ff.], Zedekiah. Or one may despise [the offense before one preaches against it] as did Shadrach, Meshach, and Abednego [Dan. 3:8ff.,

21. Exod. 23:24; Deut. 7:5, 25ff.; Jer. 4:1, and others are cited by Karlstadt in the section omitted.

esp. v. 16], and many others. For although Paul and Barnabas preached briefly, we are not therefore bound by their example even if they had preached at great length and often beforehand. For Christ's example is certainly as strong as their example. Christ drove the traders out of the temple at the same time that he said: Why do you make my father's house [96] a den of murderers? And a house of commerce [Matt. 21:12–13; John 2:14–22]?

If you seek God's commands and teaching, you will find this: "Destroy all places where the heathen (whom you will conquer) have served their gods, whether on the high hills and mountains or under green trees, and pull them down, devastate, and do away with them" [Deut. 12:2–3]. God has not commanded the Jews to preach to the heathen before they did away with their idols. And what are our idolatrous Christians except twofold heathen? Therefore it is unnecessary for one to teach them before one takes their destruction away from them. Even if they become angry, they will no doubt laugh afterward. God has not commanded the Jews to do this in the whole world, but rather in the places which they would conquer and in which they would rule.

The conclusion therefore is this: Where Christians rule, there they should consider no government, but rather freely on their own hew down and throw down what is contrary to God, even without preaching. Such offenses are numerous—for example, the mass, images, the idolatrous flesh which the priests now devour, etc. However, when something is grounded in God's figurative sayings,[22] then one should preach and point out the concealed, unchanging will of God before one acts contrary to any Scripture; or [one should preach] and announce reasons for the new example at the same time or soon afterward if there are people present who might take offense at the example contrary to Scripture.[23] That is what Christ did when his disciples broke the sabbath according to the external letter and appearance; and Stephen when he belittled the temple; and Peter when he baptized Cornelius; and Paul when he spoke and acted against circumcision; etc. All these exegeted the law of God as the prophets had done. In this situation, therefore, Paul wants one to spare the weak, that is, the ignorant. Here, how-

22. See n. 12 above.
23. That is, contrary to the literal sense of Scripture (see n. 12 above).

ever, I want to ask: Why did Paul not allow the Galatians to be circumcised until they and others became sufficiently strong and informed? However, one may certainly break human traditions when they have no plant of divine truth, although one suppresses them with nothing other than the word of Christ: "Every plant which my father has not planted will be rooted out" [Matt. 15:13]. Human laws are the dung which the Jews had to carry outside their tents and bury with earth. That which God forbids and which makes one sin against him and which destroys the neighbor, one should take away immediately, the sooner the better. For [97] thereby one serves God and does good to the neighbor, even though he grumbles and scolds because of it. And one brings him to consider what is best for him. To that end, may God help us. Amen.

I want to make a separate little book about the multiplicity of offenses because I see that it is necessary.[24] In it, I want to point out clearly that those who daily cry, "Spare the weak from offense" lie in the midst of offense and offend the sick the most.

24. See p. 64, n. 17.

5

A Radical View of the Lord's Supper: Karlstadt's *Concerning the Anti-Christian Misuse of the Lord's Bread and Cup*

Accepting Luther's challenge to attack his eucharistic doctrine, Karlstadt sent his brother-in-law to Switzerland in the fall of 1524 with five radical tracts on the Lord's Supper. In them Karlstadt rejected more than a millennium of Christian eucharistic theology. He developed a purely symbolic understanding of the eucharistic presence of Christ and denounced every vestige of the sacrament as a means of grace.* Directed primarily against Luther, these five tracts contain the first published Protestant enunciation of a symbolic eucharistic doctrine. They constitute, in fact, the first salvo in a long, bitter intra-Protestant battle over the meaning of the Eucharist.

Concerning the Anti-Christian Misuse of the Lord's Bread and Cup, translated in full here, summarizes most of Karlstadt's eucharistic thinking without the tedious exegesis of some of the other four eucharistic tracts.† Here as in all his writings on the Lord's Supper, Karlstadt vividly underlines the centrality of the cross. Particularly striking is his complete reversal of his earlier attitude‡ toward the necessity of preparation for partaking of the Eucharist. This work

* For an extensive discussion of Karlstadt's eucharistic theology, see Crerar Douglas, "The Coherence of Andreas Bodenstein von Karlstadt's Early Evangelical Doctrine of the Lord's Supper; 1521–1525" (Ph.D. dissertation, Hartford Seminary Foundation, 1973). Karlstadt's exegesis paralleled that of the thirteenth century Waldensians at some points (*LW* 40, 154, n. 114). A symbolic interpretation, developed in Holland, was known at Wittenberg in 1521; see George H. Williams, *The Radical Reformation* (Philadelphia: Westminster, 1962), pp. 27–37.

† *Dialogus oder ein gesprechbüchlin von dem grewlichen unnd abgöttischen missbrauch des hochwirdigsten sacraments Jesu Christi*, the longest and best known of Karlstadt's eucharistic tracts, is in Hertzsch 2, 5–49 and *St. L* 20, 2312–59. *Wider die alte und newe papistiche Messen* is in *St. L.* 20, 2306–13. There are no modern reprints of the other two (Freys-Barge, Nos. 124–25 and 129–30).

‡ See above, pp. 7–15.

also illustrates his adaptation of mystical terminology and his vigorous concern for a truly regenerate life of obedience.

For a discussion of Karlstadt's eucharistic theology, see Gordon Rupp, *Patterns of Reformation* (Philadelphia: Fortress, 1969), pp. 141–48; *ABK*-B 2, 144ff.; Douglas, "The Coherence of Andreas Bodenstein von Karlstadt's Early Evangelical Doctrine of the Lord's Supper: 1521–1525."

The following translation is from the second edition of 1524 (Freys-Barge, No. 136) printed at Nürnberg. A modern German text is in *St. L.* 20, 92ff.

Concerning the Anti-Christian Misuse of the Lord's Bread and Cup Whether Faith in the Sacrament Forgives Sin; and Whether the Sacrament is an Arrabo[1] *or Pledge of the Forgiveness of Sin. Exegesis of the Eleventh Chapter of the First Epistle of Paul to the Corinthians, Concerning the Lord's Supper*

Andreas Karlstadt
1524

I (Aii), Andreas Bodenstein von Karlstadt, publicly confess and make known to everyone that because of dreadful error and for the sake of poor deceived Christendom, I can no longer conceal the fact that many Christians take the bread and cup of the Lord to their great injury, and harm themselves by their blind and unworthy use of the magnificent Supper and make themselves guilty of Christ's death, and forfeit the great righteousness of Christ which Christ had and communicated to all believers. Therefore, I must speak my mind and censure myself for my former writing on the sacrament[2] and relate the truth—even though others, who are considered the princes of the biblical scholars, should properly have done it before me, and even though they would like us so tied to themselves that we would neither write nor undertake any action until they do.[3] But since they hide it behind the bush and dig ditches or hide pointed sticks for simple people, I must nevertheless confess God's truth and the lofty righteousness of Christ, whether it means life or death.

As your servant, I pray that none of you will look at me or any other person, but rather that each one will pay attention to his inner witness of the Spirit. But if he needs the external and scriptural witness for himself or another I pray that he will look

1. *Arrabo* and *arra* are the Latin for the Greek word *arrabon*, which in turn goes back to a Hebrew word which means "first installment, deposit, down payment or pledge" (cf. Gen. 38:17–20).

2. See below, n. 5, above, Chap. 1, and *ABK*-S, pp. 140ff. for Karlstadt's earlier views.

3. A reference to Karlstadt's conflicts with Luther; see above, pp. 2–4, 36–48, and below, pp. 149–57.

without any presuppositions at the Scripture which I will adduce.[4] For I always lead them from myself to God's genuine view, as John did who said: He is the one; I am not. He stands in your midst, but you do not recognize him [cf. John 1:20, 26]. If one finds that this instruction is right and that he is helped out of his danger, let him praise God and grasp the truth. But if there is anyone to whom this admonition is displeasing, he is free to instruct me and dedicate something better to the world. I also want to beg each person to whom it may seem good to teach me, if I go astray, either amicably or even with sharp words so that I may recognize alleged error and be corrected if God grants me grace.

When [AiiV] I call the Lord's bread and cup a sacrament, no one should therefore think that I have read that term in Scripture, but rather that I want to babble with children so that they understand me.

Whether the Sacrament Forgives Sin

It is a common and dreadful injury that our Christians seek forgiveness of sins in the sacrament.

For example, when their conscience, as they say, frightens or distresses them because of their sin, then they dispatch themselves to receive it, [and] they become content through a false illusion and trust, which I will call false until they point out a word of their faith in Scripture in which they trust.[5] For faith comes from hearing the sermon, but preaching is from the Word of God (Rom. 10 [:17]). Therefore, no one should give credence to them until they preach a word of faith and point out that the Lord's bread is a sacrament or forgives sin. And when they have preached and pointed out a word of true faith, then you shall be dependent on the naked truth and not on their persons. From their speech you must grasp whether they advance true and divine things.

That faith which reflects or portrays a thing to oneself as one wants to have it is a bewitched faith and fundamentally a false light and irrational knowledge. Faith in Christ must direct itself according to the manner of Christ. It must recognize Christ just

4. For a discussion of the spiritualist implications of this and one other similar comment, see *ABK-S*, pp. 268–72.

5. Karlstadt here attacks Luther's view that the sacrament strengthens faith, a view which Karlstadt himself also accepted in 1521 (see above, pp. 8–10, 13–14 and *ABK-S*, p. 142, esp. n. 177 where references to Luther are given).

as he is, not make Christ into whatever one wants. Otherwise faith would present one with a fictitious image. And if one had known and believed for a long time, one would nevertheless not know that one believed in a false and invented thing. Therefore I say that he who manufactures peace and forgiveness of sins for his conscience via that which God has not established for peace and forgiveness of sins consequently does not have peace and forgiveness of sins [Aiii] because he pacifies himself with a false consolation. Rather, he will and must be confounded eventually, although he stands peacefully for a while.

Accordingly, all men who, without the word of faith, attribute to the sacrament peace for their conscience and forgiveness for their sins, or who make the sacrament a pledge which is to assure our consciences, must be confounded and mocked (II Cor. 1 [:22]; Eph. 1 [:14]). For they do not find a letter of that in the words of faith.

Because that is not right, I will briefly take in hand and treat Paul's teaching which he has written concerning the worthy use of the Lord's bread and cup in I Cor. 11. For I have written very widely of this matter in a dialogue and elsewhere in other books.[6]

Paul says why, how, and when we enjoy the Lord's bread and cup worthily and beneficially and writes exactly what the prophets and apostles have written about the knowledge of Christ's body and blood.

He who teaches otherwise or brings forward another gospel is banned and accursed and his teaching is also a banned, dreadful, and accursed teaching (Gal. 1 [:8, 9]).

The text: I Cor. 11 [:26] says: "As often as you eat of this bread and drink of this cup, you proclaim the Lord's death until he comes."

Each person should consider this form and manner and eat the Lord's bread and drink of the cup accordingly. For Paul has given it as a rule by which all people who want to partake of the Lord's Supper must be governed.

One [AiiiV] should notice, however, that this proclamation is a fruit of a tree, namely, of the remembrance of the body and blood

6. See above, p. 72, n. †.

of Christ concerning which indeed Paul had just spoken above and had just introduced the words of the Lord Jesus Christ. For everything that happens through external words or things must flow out of the ground of the heart[7] and be accomplished rightly in inwardness. God judges the heart, and the inward man is a cherished good and a noble thing in God's eyes when it is prepared as God wants to have it prepared.

Therefore God says through Isaiah and also through Christ himself: "The people praise me with their mouth but their heart is far from me" (Isa. 29 [:13]; Matt. 15 [:8]). Hence the proclamation, if it is righteous, must flow forth from a good, concealed fountain. Paul pointed out the same fountain and ground to the Romans when he said: He who believes from the heart is justified, but with the mouth one confesses for salvation (Rom. 10 [:10]).

It is totally impossible for any external thing whatsoever to be righteous or correct if the heart is not justified beforehand. For it stands written: "He who does not have a justified soul within himself is an unbeliever" (Hab. 2 [:4]). To unbelievers, all things are impure and defiled (Tit. 1 [:15]).

On the other hand, to believers, all things are pure, good, and righteous. The eyes of God look upon faith (Jer. 5 [:3]). If a man has a righteous heart and upright spirit, then he pleases God and his external confession also pleases God. Therefore I say that the proclamation of Christ's death, which is an external work or thing, must sprout from a concealed and hidden heart if it is good and pleasing to God.

Hence we must seek the same ground on[8] which the external, proper proclamation of Christ's death stands. The ground, however, is easily found when you yearn for it. Nor did Paul want to leave it unmentioned. "What is that selfsame ground?" you ask. The answer is: "The remembrance."

"For [Aiv] the Lord Jesus in the night he was betrayed, took bread and gave thanks and broke it and said, 'Take, eat, this is my body which is broken for you. Do this in remembrance of me.' Likewise also he took the cup after supper and said, 'This cup is

7. For a discussion of Karlstadt's use of mystical terminology such as "ground of the soul," used interchangeably with "ground of the heart," see *ABK-S*, pp. 213ff. esp. pp. 230–36.

8. Reading *auf* for *auss* (with *St. L.*).

the new testament in my blood. Do this, as often as you drink, in remembrance of me'" (I Cor. 11 [:23–25]).

There Paul establishes the ground of the proclamation of Christ's death out of which flows this fruit of our lips, namely, the proclamation which edifies and improves other people and therefore is called a confession for salvation.

Now he who wants to proclaim or confess the death of Christ externally in a proper way must above all have gone into his ground[9] and must proceed from the ground or inwardness. And his heart must give birth to this fruit of his lips, that is, the proclamation, as a tree bears its fruit from the roots.

What Remembrance Is

The remembrance, however, is a passionate and loving knowledge or perception of the body and blood of Christ. For indeed no one can remember what he has not perceived.

The perception, however, must be formed by and coincide with the object,[10] that is, one must perceive the body and the blood of Christ in the same manner and with the same intentions as Christ gave his body and shed his blood for our sins (Gal. 1 [:4]).

Therefore, Christ said clearly: Eat the bread, for this body is the body which is given to you;[11] and this is my blood which must be shed for you. It is as if he intended to say (although the disciples learned it first on Pentecost): "Moses and the prophets have written to you and all men of a body which must be given for you, which would be a seed of a woman and would tread upon the snake's head (Gen. 3 [:15]), [and] would also stretch out its hand to the wood of life. My [AivV] body, or this my body, is the very one which they all prophesied must be given for the world. Therefore you shall eat my bread in remembrance of me." Likewise of his blood Christ said, or intended to say: "Moses and the prophets have written of blood which will make a new testament and must be shed for sins. Notice! My blood is the very blood which must be shed for you for the forgiveness of sins." Anyone

9. That is, his heart. See the following sentence and n. 7 above.

10. *Gegenwurff* is the equivalent of *Objekt* (Götze).

11. This passage presupposes Karlstadt's particular exegesis of the words of institution. He believed that when Christ said the words "This is my body," he pointed not to the bread but to himself, that is, his body. It was this body which the prophets foretold. See, e.g., *Dialogus*, Hertzsch 2, 15–17 (esp. p. 17).

who wants to have a proper remembrance and a blameless proclamation of Christ's death must perceive the offered body of Christ and his shed blood in this manner. If the remembrance is not directed in this manner, then it is not faithful to Moses and all the prophets to whom Christ constantly points and says: Christ had to suffer, shed his blood, die, rise again, and thus enter into his glory, as it stands written in the prophets (Luke 24 [:26]).

Those who have the proper knowledge of Christ have righteousness in their ground. As Paul says, faith is the righteousness of the heart (Rom. 10 [:10]). Yes, that is true, if it is not a frozen or dead understanding, but rather an ardent, passionate, industrious, powerful knowledge of Christ which transforms the perceiver into the perceived life and death of Christ and desires to do or forsake for Christ's sake all that Christ wants. However, Isaiah points out that righteous faith in Christ is an understanding of Christ's death and his intentions when he first depicts the surrendered body of the Messiah with his peculiar form and then says: In his knowledge, or understanding, the righteous one will make many of his servants righteous [Isa. 53:11].

You ask: "When and in what form is Christ known so that his knowledge and understanding shall justify?" My answer is: Consider Isaiah, and you will find that Christ was offered up to death as a lamb because he so desired; [you will also find] that he was wounded for our sins and was held as a despised and accursed one whom God had rejected. And although Isaiah has presented Christ thus crucified, he says, "In [B] his knowledge, will he make righteous," because the Christ thus mocked, wounded, and hanged makes righteous. That is what Christ says: The Son of Man must be lifted up so that each person who looks at the one suspended, or believes on him, is saved and does not perish (John 3 [:14–15]). That is what Paul says: Through one man's obedience many men have become righteous (Rom. 4 [5:19]). Understand obedience from the passage where it is written: He has become obedient even unto death (Phil. 3 [2:8]). Consequently, in the obedience of the death which he suffered, he has brought the name of Jesus into the highest state of all, so that Christ is called a Savior. That is the reason that Paul values and prizes the surpassing knowledge of Christ so highly, and says that righteousness comes only through knowledge of Jesus Christ, and announces very precisely that the righteousness which comes from God stands in the knowledge of Christ and in the power of his resurrection and in the fellowship of his suffering so that one becomes similar to and like his death [Phil. 3:9ff.]. Therefore Paul also writes: I know nothing except Jesus the crucified. From this it follows that the knowledge of the hanged Jesus makes righteous.

Briefly, the perception or knowledge of the body of Christ which was given and of his blood which was shed is the first reason which should move [you] to take the Lord's Supper. You must look there again so that you do not make the body and blood of the Lord mere flesh which is not useful at all. You must have before your eyes and understand the great invisible love, the surpassing obedience, the excellent innocence of Christ, etc. And you must understand these things in the depths of your heart. Then you will be justified, redeemed from sin. And thus you must hold the words of Christ, "This is my body" (concerning which it was prophesied) "which must be given for you," as the genuine and joyful gospel which all apostles proclaim. Formerly that was a promise; now it no longer is a promise but rather has been fulfilled in Christ [and] has become a clear gospel, as Paul says. Long ago Moses wrote of the body and blood of Christ. Prophets promised the body which would be given for us. However, [BV] the apostles and we preach the joyful message of the surrendered body and shed blood of Jesus Christ of which Christ spoke before his death.

From the knowledge of Christ arises that remembrance of Christ which is not a coarse, cold, and lazy remembrance, but rather a fresh, passionate, and powerful remembrance, which makes or gives joy, which dearly esteems, highly prizes, and gives thanks for the surrendered body and shed blood of Christ, and which makes Christ-like and makes one ashamed of all that is contrary to Christ.

Take an example of that. If you had had to die on the gallows or wheel or in the fire and the sentence had already been spoken against you and you had to go to death and one came who would die for you and free you through his death, would you not be eternally ashamed if you did something that you should not do because of your love for such a good friend? And on the other hand, would you not be happy when his name was well spoken of?

Would you not speak well of him eternally? And if at the end he left something for you that you were to use in remembrance of him, would you not use the same with fresh, passionate remembrance? And with a horror of yourself for having done such a deed for which you would justly have been put to death if the innocent one had not taken your guilt upon himself and paid for it with his death? In the same way, we should also retain the remembrance of the Lord, understand from our heart, and remember that Christ gave his body in death and shed his blood for us—innocently, out of great love, out of incomparable obedience.

The remembrance of Christ has two parts. The one is because of the body which was given, the other because of the blood which was shed.[12]

Now he who wants to enjoy the Lord's Supper must consider and know the reasons why our Lord Christ shed his blood and gave his body for us, together with the fruit, as the apostles and disciples of Christ, after Easter when they received the Holy Spirit, knew the reasons for the surrendered body and the shed blood of Christ which [Bii] the books of the apostles, Acts, and the letter to the Hebrews report. See how Christ has become a sacrifice and a priest, [and] why he offered himself (Heb. 6, 10). Then you will certainly discover that we all have obtained forgiveness of our sins and righteousness through one sacrifice, one death, one body, one obedience, one innocence, one holiness, one redemption, one cleansing.

Therefore, it is not true that the sacrament forgives sins for us. It is against Moses, prophets, apostles, and Christ. In addition, it is a reproach against the suffering and great obedience of Christ. Thus those who seek the forgiveness of their sins in the sacrament are perhaps as foolish and evil as the priests who sacrifice Christ daily for new sins. At least they are almost that evil. When Christ's obedience is perceived or Christ's will (which was the will of the father) is understood, it is our justification, and it purifies the heart and forgives guilt. We want to see that more properly when we deal with the text at greater length.

12. Already in 1521 Karlstadt had developed this idea, perhaps to reinforce the reformers' attack on the medieval practice of giving only the bread to the laity (see *ABK*-S, p. 144, and Chap. 1, pp. 9–11).

It has been pointed out now that the proclamation of the death of Christ must flow out of the remembrance of Christ, and the remembrance of Christ must flow out of the perception of the surrendered body and shed blood of Christ. And it has been pointed out that we must know the reasons, powers, and fruits of the crucified body together with those of the shed blood of Christ if the proclamation is to be correct, so that it is not our own wisdom and thoughts which are found in us. Beware of the judgment of Christ, who said [cf. Luke 24:25]: O you fools, do you not believe what the prophets and Moses have written about me? Concerning the body and blood of Christ, they have written that Christ would wash away our sins in his body and with his blood. Concerning the sacrament which forgives sins, no one has written. Concerning the body which would be hanged on the cross, Christ has also said to us that he was to pay for our sins. But no prophet, nor Christ, nor even any Christian brother has written that Christ forgives sins in the sacrament. For if it could be that Christ forgives sin for us in the sacrament, it would follow that we would have to perceive Christ not on the cross but rather in the sacrament, and that Christ has not forgiven sin for us through his body [and] also that his death was not sufficiently powerful.

However, [BiiV] that is to trample upon Christ with one's feet, to reproach and to give the lie to God the Father. Let anyone show me one little letter [of Scripture which indicates] that the sacramental essence of the body and blood is useful to us in the sacrament for the forgiveness of sins. Christ says: My blood is shed for the forgiveness of sins. So I ask: Is the blood poured out in the sacrament or on the cross? If it is poured out in the sacrament, then the boast of the cross of Christ is invalidated and false, and Paul, who boasted of nothing except Christ's cross, has become a coward. If it is poured out on the cross, then we must direct our perception to the cross and not to the sacrament. We are truly anti-Christians, defamers and despisers of Christ's passion, to the extent that we ascribe to our sacrament what belongs to Christ on the cross. Christ says: Do that in remembrance of me. But they say: You shall remember the body in the sacrament. And yet they cannot point out one little hair of Scripture through which we could understand how the body and blood of Christ are to be in the sacrament or why they are to be there.

Paul says: As often as you eat of the Lord's bread, and drink of his cup, you shall proclaim the Lord's death. On the contrary, they teach thus: You shall believe that Christ is in the sacrament. You shall believe that the sacrament forgives your sins. You shall believe that the sacrament is a sure pledge of forgiveness of sins and your holiness. And they drive four in hand into a dreadful contradiction of the righteousness, love, innocence, and wisdom of Christ which he has manifested through his death. Paul says: You shall speak of the Lord's death. But they say: You shall speak of the sacrament.

I have written in my *Dialogue*[13] about the meaning of "until he comes."

The text follows:

"Now [Biii] Whoever Eats This Bread and Drinks the Cup of the Lord Unworthily Is Guilty of the Body and Blood of the Lord" (I Cor. 11 [:27])

Christ indicated the guilt when he said: "The Son of Man goes as it is written of him, but woe to him through whom he is betrayed" (Matt. 26 [:24]). Peter says: You have murdered the Lord of life and denied and cast away your Savior (Acts 2 [3:14–15]). He who partakes of the Lord's Supper unworthily is guilty as were the murderers of Christ who not only reproached Christ but also put him to death.

Through the following text I will unfold just what the unworthiness is and in what is consists.

The text reads thus: He who eats and drinks unworthily eats and drinks judgment on himself [I Cor. 11:29]. Why? Because he does not discern the body of the Lord. There you have the reason for the unworthiness, namely, that he who does not properly discern the Lord's body there eats and drinks unworthily. Show me a little word of where Paul says: He who does not discern the sacrament eats the Lord's bread unworthily. I know that we must discern the Lord's body. It is also true that I am to sit at the Lord's table with becoming behavior and take his bread and drink with the intention with which he offered it to me. But that I am to hold his bread and wine as himself is not commanded to me. The Lord can give me life, salvation, redemption, righteousness,

13. See above, p. 72, n. †.

and similar goods and treasures, but the bread and drinking glass can give me none of these. Therefore, I must not look to his bread or drink, but to him.

If I set heart, spirit, mind, and thought on the Lord and became enraptured with ecstasy in him, it would certainly not hurt me at all although I spilled[14] or upset some of the sacrament. Worthiness [BiiiV] lies in knowledge of him and not in his supper. Unworthiness and guilt for his death, etc., arise from lack of understanding of Christ's body and blood or from negligence which does not discern what it should discern.

This little phrase "not to discern" may also be expressed thus: "Not to judge well"; or, "Not to perceive precisely." For Paul grounds his whole teaching on the saying of Christ who said: "This is my body which is given for you. This is my blood which. . . ." And Paul wants to point out, as he does clearly in all the epistles, what Christ said: My body is the body which is given for you. And this is my blood which must be shed for you. One had to come who had to place his body and his blood there for our sakes. We must understand this very one's body and blood precisely if we intend somehow to escape damnation and be saved. We must eat his flesh and drink his blood (John 6 [:53]) and must know that we cannot be saved without knowledge, decision, judgment, or discernment of him.

He who does not differentiate in this way the body of Christ from all other bodies and does not distinguish it from all bodies and in the meantime eats of the Lord's table is guilty of his death and deserves judgment. For Christ has given us his bread to eat and his cup to drink with the intention that we remember him.

He who remembers, however, must understand the Word of the Lord when he says: This is my body, etc.; this is my blood, etc. He who does not understand also does not remember, or does not always remember the Lord as he should remember him. If he does not remember, then he does not discern the body of the Lord and he does not esteem Christ's body and treasure the body so greatly and highly as he should treasure it. Therefore, he becomes guilty first and foremost when he eats the Lord's bread and drinks from the Lord's cup and does not perceive the Lord's body and blood.

14. *Verreren* is the equivalent of *vergiessen* (Götze).

Now I ask: Where are we to discern, precisely determine, and properly judge the Lord's body? If you answer, "In the sacrament," then [Biv] I ask: Did Christ die in the sacrament? Has Christ given his soul for us in the sacrament? Where was that great and wide piece of bread in which Christ stood with his cross and the great mocking crowd? If the Jews and heathen mocked Christ in the sacrament, must they not always have been with him in it? Likewise, both thieves with their crosses, bodies and words would have been in it. If Christ was obedient to his father even unto death in the sacrament, why did his disciples not flee from him when he gave them his bread and cup as they fled when they captured Christ? Was Christ sacrificed outside the gates of Jerusalem or in the city of Jerusalem where they ate the sacrament? Had the betrayer given Christ into the hands of the Jews when Christ sat at table with the disciples or did he surrender him afterward?

I maintain that no one may say that Christ has given his body in the sacrament for our sins. For one of the following must fall and come to naught: either that Christ has given his body for us in the sacrament, or that Christ has given his body in death for us on the cross. The second, however, is truly foretold by Moses, by the prophets, especially by Isaiah, and subsequently most clearly and often by Christ. Therefore, the first must be false (as it is) and come to naught. Also, if the first were maintained, almost all the apostles' writings would fall and an eternal mockery would result.

Since we must judge, or determine and properly discern the body of the Lord, not as he is in the sacrament, but as he offered his body as a sin offering, a food offering, a heave and wave offering[15] to his father of his free will and showed the greatest innocence, highest obedience, and ecstatic love, it follows that they who do not look back to and lift their eyes to the figurative, suspended snake,[16] but rather only take notice of the sacrament so that they receive Christ with the sacrament, have taken the Lord's bread and cup altogether unworthily and have made themselves [BivV] guilty of the death of Jesus Christ and deserve judgment. It would

15. Different types of offerings prescribed in the Pentateuch—e.g., Exod. 29:26–28.

16. That is, Christ, of which the snake elevated by Moses was a prefiguration (cf. John 3:14–15; Num. 21:8–9).

be better for them if they would eat figs instead. The Lord's body is the promised body which was to carry away the world's sins through his suffering and death. Therefore Christ wanted us, when we want to eat his bread, to remember and to have understood all that was written about him—that is, how he was to be wounded for our redemption, etc. Paul names only the body here [v. 29] not so that we should perceive the Lord's blood without determining, judging, and discerning it, and should not prize it above all blood. Rather, by the body we must also understand that we should discern the Lord's blood if we do not want to become guilty of his blood. Therefore Paul has named both body and blood [v. 27].

If we held such an earnest understanding of the body and blood of Christ, then none of us would eat himself full or get drunk as the foolish Corinthians did. Instead each one would refrain from all kinds of vices which are against Christ or bring him into disgrace. Each person, therefore should examine himself sufficiently beforehand, and, as it is said, so eat of the Lord's bread and drink of the cup.

To examine means to perceive with certainty, that is, to learn. Paul has used the word in the Greek tongue in many places (Rom. 5 [2:18], 12 [:2], I Thess. 5 [:21]). And it always means truly to learn, to understand with certainty in the sense in which I John 4 [:1] uses it when he says: Discern the spirits beforehand, whether they are of God. Paul places the responsibility in each home and in the very own breast of each person, and desires that each and every person should examine himself, that is, understand from assured learning whether or not he perceives the body and the blood of Christ, which the prophets promised, with a knowledge which is rich in love[17] and which esteems Christ highly.

For if he has the worthy and passionate knowledge of the body of Christ which has borne our sins with great bitterness and mockery, and [C] of the blood which has washed him of his evil works and sins, then he becomes Christ-like and thankful for the passion, sober, well-behaved, wise, reasonable, discreet. And he will certainly keep himself from the evil practices of the Corinthians who drank themselves full. Because of the Lord's table, he will

17. Karlstadt often spoke of "faith [or knowledge] rich in love" and "love rich in faith." See *ABK-S*, pp. 236–38.

also sit with decorum. Certainly he will see to it that he does not take the Lord's bread for his own pleasure, or for bodily satisfaction, and also not as any other bread, or without knowledge of him who has given it to him to eat in remembrance of himself.

This examination consists of inwardness and looks right into the ground of the soul[18] where God acts and produces his gifts. Therefore Paul leads each person to himself and not to another man as the papists have done. They direct the partakers of Christ's Supper to poor blind leaders who call themselves father confessors. But Paul was more intelligent in the matter and led each one to himself, into his inwardness. For no man knows what is in a man's spirit except the spirit of each man.

When you want to take the Lord's Supper, you should go into your inwardness and not perceive superficially whether you have a sincere and worthy remembrance of Christ so that you may take it, but rather experience an awareness, that is, a certain knowledge of yourself that you are as Christ would have you.

The Sacrament Is No Arrabo, Arra,[19] *Pledge, or Farthing of God*

This statement of Paul, that is, "Each one should examine himself," etc., demolishes another commonly expressed statement, namely, that the bread and the cup of Christ are an assurance and a certain voucher by which one can be certain and sure in himself that Christ's death has brought [CV] redemption for him. For if one could or should be certain of his redemption, that is, the forgiveness of sins, through the Supper, it would be unnecessary for each person to examine himself before he took the Lord's bread and cup. It would be enough for him to feel and understand whether he were fit as God would have him. But that is against Christ who says: Do that in remembrance of me, that is, take my bread and my cup in remembrance of me—the bread for a remembrance that I gave my body for you, the cup for a remembrance of my shed blood. Beforehand, therefore, before he takes it, each person is to examine himself to see whether or not he has the remembrance of Christ. If he has it, then he is also certain of his redemption and has a peace with God through Christ (Rom. 5 [:1]), not through

18. See n. 7 above.
19. See n. 1 above.

the sacrament, and he may take it joyfully. If he does not have it, and does not find in himself that he has an assured perception of his redemption, then he is not fit as Christ wants him who eats his supper to be fit. Just as little fit was that one who had no wedding garment on to sit at the king's table (Matt. 22 [:11]). Therefore, he should stay away from the Lord's meal so that he is not guilty and is not cast into outer darkness as that one was. However, that this certainty should be in those who want to take the Lord's Supper before they partake, and does not happen to us and come through the bread and cup which some call a sign, Paul has clearly and abundantly pointed out when he said: You shall examine yourself and so eat of the bread, etc. [I Cor. 11:28].

What does the little phrase "and so" mean? Does it not mean that he should examine himself beforehand and truly understand whether he has a remembrance of the Lord and can proclaim the Lord's death with the intention, will, and manner that Christ desires? If he has that in his ground, then he also has the Spirit of Christ who shows to him Christ his Savior hanging on the cross, and also shows the same Christ dying in full obedience, sublime righteousness, ecstatic love, and innocence. And the Spirit assures his heart that he has redemption through Christ.

If [Cii] he has this assurance of the Spirit of Christ, which he must have, then he may so eat of the Lord's bread and drink of his cup. But he so eats and drinks when he is already assured and certain, before he receives the sacrament, that Christ has paid and borne the sins of all the world.

Christ always directs us all to himself on the cross where he obediently died and accomplished everything which was written about him. We look at him there with blessed eyes, that is, believe in him and know with certainty that he redeemed us, etc. When we know that and so look back upon the death which Christ suffered, then we are inwardly justified and are indeed worthy to eat and drink of the Lord's bread and wine. Also, when we discover that we are such knowers and rememberers, then we may eat and drink joyfully. That is why he says: "Let a man examine himself beforehand and so." The word "so" means fitness and time. Fitness relates to the remembrance. Time relates to the fact that the fitness must precede, just as one must have a wedding garment before one goes to a king's table.

Now even though I would elsewhere confess[20] and admit that one can experience and become certain of God's promise or work through some signs, when they [the signs] are so much beyond rational comprehension that the soul secretly comes to know a sublime power of God because of astonishment over the signs which occur, just as Hezekiah came to know God's power and will through the backward movement of the sun [Isa. 38:8], nevertheless, it is neither certain nor good for us to give or ascribe to the bread and wine of Christ what belongs properly to Christ and the Spirit of Christ. Christ is the way, truth, life, and peace; and we have all that through Christ.

Now he who ascribes these goods to the Supper, to the bread and wine of the Lord, does nothing other than attack Christ in his treasure and confer on a creature smaller than himself what is only of Christ and what Christ alone bestows.

He [CiiV] who does not enter through Christ is always a thief and a murderer. That would mean to enter through bread or wine and not through Christ. Or at least it would mean to enter not only through Christ, but rather through both Christ and his Supper. Christ, however, hates that, for he wants to have a whole heart, which in the previous case would be almost split apart and not whole.

If Christ is our peace and assurance, how can soulless creatures assure us and make us certain? His blood, that is, the passionate knowledge of the shed blood of Christ, washes us and our consciences from dead works.

But if the blood can do that, then it must also assure us as it indeed does when it is known. But if the cup does that, then the cup which we take today was previously shed for our sins before it grew on the vine.

The deficiency lies in the perception. And in this case, therefore, Christ did not want to give us a sign which would make our powers and soul move (just as elsewhere he does work which no one else has done) so that we would ascribe to him alone, and not to the signs, what many foolish people now grant to the soulless signs. Christ has promised to send us his Holy Spirit. And he prophesied: When he comes, he will tell you all things, and he will

20. See above, n. 5.

bear witness to you and you will bear witness of me (Rom. 8).[21] See there, the Spirit of Christ gives us the witness that he gave his body for us and shed his blood for us.

Now since that belongs to the Holy Spirit, it is sacrilege and wantonness for us to ascribe that to the bread or wine. Indeed, it is a robbery in which one steals from the Holy Spirit his proper work and special attributes and ascribes them to a poor creature and thereby establishes a new idolatry. The childlike Spirit which makes us cry "Abba, Father" (Rom. 8 [:15–17]) assures our spirit, etc.

The sacrament does not make us cry to God, "Father, Father." For it is much too coarse to touch, not to mention teach, the ground of the soul. Now if the bread or the cup does not teach us [Ciii] to cry to God, "'Father, Father" (which we nevertheless must do in the passion of Christ if we understand rightly), the sacrament cannot assure our spirit nor help the weakness of our spirit. For such calling and assurance belong to a master workman. The assurance belongs to God's Spirit and not to any creature. The Spirit of Christ anoints us. He seals us. He is the pledge of our redemption (II Cor. 1 [:22]; Eph. 1 [:14]). Since it belongs to the Spirit of God to assure our spirit and to make us certain of our redemption, one should hurry to the Spirit, yearn to learn from him, and receive through the Spirit what pertains to the Spirit which also no one other than the Spirit can give—namely, the assurance of forgiven sins.

If it were harmless for us to seek so sublime a thing in creaturely things such as the sacrament (i.e., the bread and wine of Christ), undoubtedly Christ would have been wise enough to have been able to tell us that and also gracious enough not by any means to have withheld the same from us. For Christ commanded his disciples to go into the world and preach that people keep all that he commanded (Matt. 28 [:20]). And Paul says that Scripture is rich and adequate.

Since therefore no Scripture can be found which asserts that we are to be assured or confirmed through the Lord's bread or wine, or that we are to learn of our redemption from it, it is an

21. Cf. John 14:25–26; 15:26–27. The reference to Romans appears to be a mistake.

addition contrary to Scripture and is to be shunned as a blasphemy against the Spirit of God and Christ.

He who has rightly understood me cannot conclude that I bring such new things to light for the sake of curiosity or to obtain fame. But if I do that, God will be my judge. But I must confess that I almost rather fear being silent.

For I know that I will suffer calumny and persecution for it, especially from those who want to be considered good evangelical people. However, because it concerns the surpassing obedience of Christ, because it involves the death and passion of Christ, because the gospel of Christ is reviled through the illusion which we now hear preached in all churches and because the death [CiiiV] of Christ is belittled and Christ's righteousness is brought to naught or at least declared insufficient (developments which I and all Christians should prevent, each in his own way), I must therefore break loose and point the Christians to the genuine gospel which all apostles have preached. And they have broken the Lord's bread only in remembrance and confession of Christ's death and therefore have partaken after the sermon was given. God wants to grant us grace that we understand the genuine gospel concerning Jesus of Nazareth. For that very gospel is still almost concealed and held in dishonor, and very nearly denied in the administration of all sacraments concerning which, moreover, nothing has been properly preached for hundreds of years.

6
Theological Confrontation: Luther's *Against the Heavenly Prophets*

When Karlstadt's eucharistic writings appeared in Strassburg, the leading reformers there promptly penned a letter (November 23, 1524) asking for Luther's advice. Luther quickly sent his *Letter to the Christians at Strassburg in Opposition to the Fanatic Spirit* (*LW* 40, 65–71) but this short reply was inadequate. When Karlstadt's tracts arrived in Wittenberg, Luther realized he had to reply in order to prevent the spread of what he considered dangerously heretical views of the Eucharist. Luther finished the first part of *Against the Heavenly Prophets* by the end of December 1524 and the second part a month later.

Against the Heavenly Prophets is a consummately devastating, delightfully satirical polemic. It is also violent—so violent, indeed, that even Melanchthon complained about its tone. But Luther felt that Karlstadt threatened central elements of Reformation doctrine and therefore had to be denounced vigorously.

For all its brilliance and illuminating assessment of significant theological issues, *Against the Heavenly Prophets* is not always fair. Karlstadt had not, as Luther claimed (see below, pp. 99, 112, 120), fallen back into works-righteousness or reduced the role of Christ to that of mere example. Nor is it accurate to identify Karlstadt and the Zwickau Prophets the way Luther implies (see below, p. 105, n. 18). Luther built—ignorantly one can assume—much of his case for Karlstadt's "illegal" move to the Orlamünde pastorate on misinformation.

Particularly interesting and still relevant is Luther's penetrating critique (below, pp. 119–23) of what today we would call Karlstadt's pietistic emphasis on religious experience and pious feelings. But if, where Luther could see only hypocrisy and works-righteousness, we discern a piety which, while still grounded in justification by faith alone, nevertheless yearns for what John Wesley would call the "heart strangely warmed," is Luther's criticism finally justified?

For two different assessments of the validity of Luther's theological critique of Karlstadt, see Friedel Kriechbaum, *Grundzüge der Theologie Karlstadts* (Hamburg-Bergstedt: Herbert Reich, 1967); and *ABK*-S, pp. 202–303.

The following selections are from the translations by Bernhard Erling (Part I) and Conrad Bergendoff (Part II) in the American edition of *Luther's Works* 40, 79–223.

Against the Heavenly Prophets in the Matter of Images and Sacraments

Martin Luther

1525

Part I

In the name of God and our dear Lord Jesus Christ. There has been a change in the weather. I had almost relaxed and thought the matter was finished; but then it suddenly arises anew and it is for me as the wise man says: "When man finishes, he must begin again" [Sirach 18:6].

Doctor Andreas Karlstadt has deserted us, and on top of that has become our worst enemy. May Christ grant that we be not alarmed, and give us his mind and courage, that we may not err and despair before the Satan who here pretends to vindicate the sacrament, but has much else in mind. For since he has not thus far been able to suppress with violence the whole doctrine of the gospel, he seeks to destroy it with cunning interpretation of Scripture.

. . . .

So our concern here should now be that we keep these two teachings far apart from each other: the one that teaches of the main articles, to govern the conscience in the spirit before God; the other, which teaches of things external or works. For more depends on the teaching of faith and a good conscience than on the teaching of good works. When works are lacking, help and counsel are at hand so that one can produce them if the teaching of faith remains firm and pure. But if the teaching of faith is placed in the background and works are put forward, then nothing can be good and there is neither counsel nor help. Then works lead to vain glory and seem to people to be something great, while God's glory disappears.

So it is with these honor-seeking prophets who do nothing but break images, destroy churches, manhandle the sacrament, and seek a new kind of mortification, that is, a self-chosen putting to death of the flesh. Thus far they have not set aright the conscience, which is nonetheless most important and most necessary in the Christian teaching, as has been said.

And if they had now altogether succeeded so that there were no more images, no churches remained, no one in the whole world held that the flesh and blood of Christ were in the sacrament and all went about in gray peasant garb,[1] what would be accomplished thereby? What did they expect to achieve by pressing, straining, and pursuing this course of action? Would they therewith have become Christian? Where would faith and love be? Should they come later? Why should they not have precedence? Fame, vainglory, and a new monkery would well thereby be achieved, as happens in all works, but the conscience would in no way be helped. Thus such false spirits do not care where faith or love is to be found, just as the pope does not care but presses on if only he can make sure of the works belonging to his obedience and laws. And when they do occur, still nothing has occurred.

Since Dr. Karlstadt pursues the same way and in so many books does not even teach what faith and love are[2] (yes, they speak derisively and disdainfully of us on this account, as though it were a minor doctrine), but stresses and emphasizes external works, let everyone be warned of him. Everyone should know that he has a perverted spirit that thinks only of murdering the conscience with laws, sin, and works, so that thereby nothing is set aright, even if everything happened that he professes in all his books, and with mouth and heart. Even rascals are able to do and teach all that he urges. Therefore something higher must be there to absolve and

1. Sometime in 1523, Karlstadt stopped wearing his academic dress and began using the felt hat and gray garb of the peasants. He urged his neighbors to call him "Brother Andreas."

2. Karlstadt wrote a treatise on each in 1524 (see *ABK-S*, pp. 202, 236ff.). For the one on love, see Hertzsch 1, 49–71. It is difficult to know precisely what works of Karlstadt Luther had read. The section of *Heavenly Prophets* printed on pp. 94–108 was probably directed against Karlstadt's *Whether One Should Proceed Slowly* (see above, Chap. 4), *Ursachen, der halben Andres Carolstadt vertrieben* (Hertzsch 2, 50–58), and *Von dem Sabbat* (Hertzsch 1, 21–47). The section on pp. 108–13 was probably directed against Karlstadt's *Wider die alte und newe papistische Messen* (*St. L.* 20, 2306–13). Part II (pp. 113–25) was directed against *Dialogus* (Hertzsch 2, 5–49).

comfort the conscience. This is the Holy Spirit, who is not acquired through breaking images or any other works, but only through the gospel and faith.

Now in order that we do not open our mouths too wide and marvel at the skill of these false spirits, and thereby abandon the main articles, and thus deceitfully be led off the track (for thereby the devil succeeds through these prophets), I will here briefly recount these articles of the Christian faith to which everyone is above all things to pay attention and hold fast.[3]

The first is the law of God, which is to be preached so that one thereby reveals and teaches how to recognize sin (Rom. 3 [:20] and 7 [:7]), as we have often shown in our writings. However, these prophets do not understand this correctly, for this means a truly spiritual preaching of the law, as Paul says in Rom. 7 [:14], and a right use of the law, as he says in I Tim. 1 [:8].

Secondly, when now sin is recognized and the law is so preached that the conscience is alarmed and humbled before God's wrath, we are then to preach the comforting word of the gospel and the forgiveness of sins, so that the conscience again may be comforted and established in the grace of God, etc.

Christ himself teaches these two articles in such an order (Luke 24 [:47]). One must preach repentance and the forgiveness of sins in his name. "And the Spirit (he says in John [16:8]) will convince the world of sin and of righteousness and of judgment." You do not find either of these two articles in this one or any other of the false prophets. They also do not understand them, and yet these are the most important and necessary articles.

Now the third is judgment, the work of putting to death the old man, as in Romans 5, 6, and 7. Here works are concerned, and also suffering and affliction, as we through our own discipline and fasting, watching, labor, etc., or through other persecution and disgrace put to death our flesh. This putting to death is also not handled correctly by these false prophets. For they do not accept what God gives them, but what they themselves choose. They wear gray garb, would be as peasants, and carry on with similar foolish nonsense.[4]

3. Karlstadt's *Review of Some of the Chief Articles* (see Chap. 7 below) contains his analysis of Luther's chief articles.

4. See Karlstadt's reply below, pp. 134–36.

In the fourth place, such works of love toward the neighbor should flow forth in meekness, patience, kindness, teaching, aid, and counsel, spiritually and bodily, free and for nothing, as Christ has dealt with us.

In the fifth and last place, we ought to proclaim the law and its works, not for the Christians, but for the crude and unbelieving. For among Christians we must use the law spiritually, as is said above, to reveal sin. But among the crude masses, on Mr. Everyman, we must use it bodily and roughly, so that they know what works of the law they are to do and what works ought to be left undone. Thus they are compelled by sword and law to be outwardly pious, much in the manner in which we control wild animals with chains and pens, so that external peace will exist among the people. To this end temporal authority is ordained, which God would have us honor and fear (Rom. 13 [:1]; I Pet. 3) [I Pet. 2:13, 17].

However, we must see to it that we retain Christian freedom and do not force such laws and works on the Christian conscience, as if one through them were upright or a sinner. Here questions are in order concerning the place which images, foods, clothing, places, persons, and all such external things, etc., ought to have. Whoever does not teach according to this order certainly does not teach correctly. From which you now see that Dr. Karlstadt and his spirits replace the highest with the lowest, the best with the least, the first with the last. Yet he would be considered the greatest spirit of all, he who has devoured the Holy Spirit feathers and all.[5]

Therefore I beg every Christian who observes how we bicker in this matter to remember that we are not dealing with important things, but with the most trivial ones. Bear in mind that the devil is eager to spruce up such minor matters, thereby drawing the attention of the people so that the truly important matters are neglected, as long as they gape in his direction. From this each one

5. An allusion to the dove, symbol of the Holy Spirit. Luther apparently believed that Karlstadt, like the Zwickau Prophets, claimed special revelation via the living voice of God (see above, p. 40, n. 7; p. 75, n. 4; and below, p. 105, n. 18). In a letter to the Saxon princes on November 6, 1524, Karlstadt said that Luther opposed him at three points: the Eucharist, baptism, and the living voice of God. He acknowledged the first two points and denied the third: "In the third [the living voice of God] Dr. Luther has invented such effeminate and foolish lies that I was completely amazed and was unwilling to write anything about it and thought it would be sufficient to let the sow choke in its own blood" (Hertzsch 2, 57).

should recognize how false and evil the spirit of Dr. Karlstadt is, who, not content to ignore and be silent concerning the great and significant articles, so inflates the least significant ones as if the salvation of the world depended more on them than on Christ himself. Also, he compels us to turn from the great important articles to minor ones, so that we with him lose time and are in danger of forgetting the main articles. Let this be the first fruit by which one is able to know this tree [Matt. 7:16-20].

So that the books, however, will not become too many, I will answer all of his with this one book. And since I have not yet written anything especially about images, this shall be the first. For while it pleases him to begin this work recklessly, he sought afterwards to mend himself and cover the shame with fig leaves.

On the Destruction of Images

I approached the task of destroying images by first tearing them out of the heart through God's Word and making them worthless and despised. This indeed took place before Dr. Karlstadt ever dreamed of destroying images. For when they are no longer in the heart, they can do no harm when seen with the eyes. But Dr. Karlstadt, who pays no attention to matters of the heart, has reversed the order by removing them from sight and leaving them in the heart. For he does not preach faith, nor can he preach it; unfortunately, only now do I see that. Which of these two forms of destroying images is best, I will let each man judge for himself.

. . . .

Furthermore, I have allowed and not forbidden the outward removal of images, so long as this takes place without rioting and uproar and is done by the proper authorities. In the world it is considered foolish to conceal the true reason for a good venture out of fear that it may fail. However, when Karlstadt disregards my spiritual and orderly putting away of images and makes me out to be only a "protector of images,"[6] this is an example of his holy and prophetic art, though I only resisted his factious, violent, and fanatical spirit.

. . . .

6. Karlstadt made this charge in *Whether One Should Proceed Slowly* (see above, p. 67).

This breaking of images has also another weakness in that they themselves do it in a disorderly way, and do not proceed with proper authority. As when their prophets stand, crying and arousing the masses, saying: heigh, hew, rip, rend, smash, dash, stab, strike, run, throw, hit the idols in the mouth! If you see a crucifix, spit in its face, etc. This is to do away with images in a Karlstadtian manner, to make the masses mad and foolish, and secretly to accustom them to revolution. Those who rush into this thing think they are now great saints, and become proud and impudent beyond all measure. When one looks at the matter more closely, one finds it is a work of the law which has taken place without the Spirit and faith. Yet it makes for pride of heart, as though they by such works had gained a special status before God. Actually this means teaching works and the free will all over again.

. . . .

Now that we are under our princes, lords, and emperors, we must outwardly obey their laws instead of the laws of Moses. We should therefore be calm and humbly petition them to put away such images. Where they will not do so we nonetheless have God's Word meanwhile, whereby they may be put out of the heart, until they are forcibly put away outwardly by those properly authorized. However, when these prophets hear this, they call it papistic and fawning[7] before princes. That they, on the other hand, arouse the disorderly masses and make them rebellious, that is not to fawn. Thus we will not be cleared of fawning until we teach the masses to kill the princes and the lords.

. . . .

However to speak evangelically of images, I say and declare that no one is obligated to break violently images even of God, but everything is free, and one does not sin if he does not break them with violence. One is obligated, however, to destroy them with the Word of God, that is, not with the law in a Karlstadtian manner, but with the gospel. This means to instruct and enlighten the conscience that it is idolatry to worship them, or to trust in them, since one is to trust alone in Christ. Beyond this let the external matters take their course. God grant that they may be

7. Müntzer, not Karlstadt, originated this taunt (*LW* 40, 90, n. 16).

destroyed, become dilapidated, or that they remain. It is all the same and makes no difference, just as when the poison has been removed from a snake.

Now I say this to keep the conscience free from mischievous laws and fictitious sins, and not because I would defend images.

. . . .

Now then, let us get to the bottom of it all and say that these teachers of sin and Mosaic prophets are not to confuse us with Moses. We don't want to see or hear Moses. How do you like that, my dear rebels? We say further, that all such Mosaic teachers deny the gospel, banish Christ, and annul the whole New Testament. I now speak as a Christian for Christians. For Moses is given to the Jewish people alone, and does not concern us Gentiles and Christians. We have our gospel and New Testament. If they can prove from them that images must be put away, we will gladly follow them. If they, however, through Moses would make us Jews, we will not endure it.

What do you think? What will become of this? It will become evident that these factious spirits understand nothing in the Scriptures, neither Moses nor Christ, and neither seek nor find anything therein but their own dreams. And our basis for this assertion is from St. Paul (I Tim. 1 [:9]), "The law is not laid down for the just" (which a Christian is). And Peter (Acts 15 [:10-11]), "Now therefore why do you make trial of God by putting a yoke upon the neck of the disciples which neither our fathers nor we have been able to bear? But we believe that we shall be saved through the grace of the Lord Jesus, just as they will." With this saying (as Paul with his) Peter abrogates for the Christian the whole of Moses with all his laws.

Yes, you say, that is perhaps true with respect to the ceremonial and the judicial law, that is, what Moses teaches about the external order of worship or of government. But the decalogue, that is, the Ten Commandments, are not abrogated. There is nothing of ceremonial and judicial law in them. I answer: I know very well that this is an old and common distinction, but it is not an intelligent one. For out of the Ten Commandments flow and depend all the other commandments and the whole of Moses.

. . . .

For it is true, and no one can deny it, that whoever keeps the law of Moses as a law of Moses, or deems it necessary to keep it, must regard the keeping of all laws as necessary, as St. Paul (Gal. 5 [:3]) concludes and says, "Every man who receives circumcision—he is bound to keep the whole law." Therefore also, whoever destroys images, or observes the sabbath (that is, whoever teaches that it must be kept), he also must let himself be circumcised and keep the whole Mosaic law.

. . . .

Would you here say, "You don't mean that the first commandment has been abrogated, for, after all, one ought to have a God? Furthermore, one ought not commit adultery, kill, steal?" Answer: I have spoken of the Mosaic law as laws of Moses. For to have a God is not alone a Mosaic law, but also a natural law, as St. Paul says (Rom. 1 [:20]), that the heathen know of the deity, that there is a God. . . .

Thus, "Thou shalt not kill, commit adultery, steal, etc.," are not Mosaic laws only, but also the natural law written in each man's heart, as St. Paul teaches (Rom. 2 [:15]). Also Christ himself (Matt. 7 [:12]) includes all of the law and the prophets in this natural law, "So whatever you wish that men would do to you, do so to them; for this is the law and the prophets." Paul does the same thing in Rom. 13 [:9], where he sums up all the commandments of Moses in the love which also the natural law teaches in the words, "Love your neighbor as yourself." Otherwise, were it not naturally written in the heart, one would have to teach and preach the law for a long time before it became the concern of conscience. The heart must also find and feel the law in itself. Otherwise it would become a matter of conscience for no one. However, the devil so blinds and possesses hearts, that they do not always feel this law. Therefore one must preach the law and impress it on the minds of people till God assists and enlightens them, so that they feel in their hearts what the Word says.

Where then the Mosaic law and the natural law are one, there the law remains and is not abrogated externally, but only through faith spiritually, which is nothing else than the fulfilling of the law (Rom. 3 [:31]). This is not the place to speak about that, and elsewhere enough has been said about it.[8] Therefore Moses' legislation about images and the sabbath, and what else goes beyond the natural law, since it is not supported by the natural law, is free, null and void, and is specifically given to the Jewish people alone. It is as when an emperor or a king makes special laws and ordinances in his territory, as the *Sachsenspiegel*[9] in Saxony, and yet common natural laws such as to honor parents, not to kill, not to commit adultery, to serve God, etc., prevail and remain in all lands. Therefore one is to let Moses be the *Sachsenspiegel* of the Jews and not to confuse us Gentiles with it, just as the *Sachsenspiegel* is not observed in France, though the natural law there is in agreement with it.[10]

Why does one then keep and teach the Ten Commandments? Answer: Because the natural laws were never so orderly and well written as by Moses. Therefore it is reasonable to follow the example of Moses.

With Respect to the Complaint of Dr. Karlstadt, That He Has Been Expelled from Saxony[11]

I have spoken about it with my young lord, Duke John Frederick[12] (that I admit) and pointed out Dr. Karlstadt's wantonness and arrogance. However since "the spirit" burns with such blinding intensity, I will here recount the reasons, some of which, indeed,

8. Cf. *De votis monasticis* (*Concerning Monastic Vows*), WA 8, 573ff.

9. Written by Eike von Repgow, knight and juryman, the *Sachsenspiegel* contains economic and social laws obtaining in and around Magdeburg and Halberstadt in the early thirteenth century. Although fourteen of its articles were condemned by Gregory XI in 1374 the book remained influential in the codification of German law until the middle of the nineteenth century (*LW* 40, 98, n. 20).

10. Luther's attitude toward the Mosaic law infuriated Karlstadt. See *Review of Some of the Chief Articles*, Hertzsch 2, 69, 99.

11. Karlstadt's repeated pleas for a public hearing were ignored. See *ABK*-S, pp. 196–97.

12. Duke John Frederick, son of John the Constant (1503–1554), later became elector of Saxony. Duke John Frederick and his father Duke John administered the part of electoral Saxony that included Orlamünde. After visiting the Saale Valley at the request of Duke John Frederick, Luther recommended Karlstadt's removal from Orlamünde, but apparently not his expulsion from Saxony. See Karl Müller, *Luther und Karlstadt* (Tübingen: Mohr, 1907), pp. 174–75.

are not known to the princes of Saxony, why I am happy that Dr. Karlstadt is out of the country. And insofar as my entreaties are effectual, he shall not again return, and would again have to leave were he to be found here, unless he become another Andrew,[13] which God grant. If God wills, I will fawn before no princes. But much less will I suffer that the rebellious and the disobedient among the masses are to be led to despise temporal authority.

. . . .

And this is my basis and reason: We have noted above how Dr. Karlstadt and image-breakers of his kind do not interpret Moses' commandment as referring to the constituted authority, as is proper, but to the disorderly populace. That is certainly not the right spirit and attitude. For, as I have said, where the populace has the right and power to carry out a divine commandment, then one must thereafter give in and permit them to carry out all the commandments. Consequently, whoever arrives on the scene first must put to death murderers, adulterers, thieves, and punish rogues. And thereby justice, jurisdiction, dominion, and all authority would fall apart. Matters would take their course in accordance with the proverb: Give a rogue an inch and he takes a mile. For why do we have sovereigns? Why do they carry the sword, if the masses are to rush in blindly and straighten things out themselves?

After that, such disorder will gain in momentum, and the masses will have to kill all of the wicked. For Moses, when he commands the people to destroy images (Deut. 7 [:16]), also commands them to destroy without mercy those who had such images in the land of Canaan.

. . . .

But, you say, Dr. Karlstadt does not want to kill. That one can see from the letters which those of Orlamünde wrote to the Allstedtians.[14] Answer: I also believed it! But I believe it no longer. I no longer ask what Dr. Karlstadt says or does. He has not hit the truth for the first time. Of the spirit which they have and which impels them, I say that it is not good and is bent on murder and rebellion. Although he bows and scrapes because he sees that

13. A play on Karlstadt's name, Andreas. In the German, "another Andrew" is "ein ander Andres" (*LW* 40, 103, n. 30).

14. See above, p. 41, n. 9.

he is in a tight spot, I shall clearly show that what I have said is so. God forbid, but suppose Dr. Karlstadt won a large following, which he thought he could assemble on the Saale,[15] and the German Bible alone was read, and Mr. Everybody began to hold this commandment (about killing the wicked) under his own nose, in what direction would Dr. Karlstadt go? How would he control the situation? Even if he had never intended to consent to something like that, he would have to follow through. The crowds would mutiny and cry and shout as obstinately, "God's Word, God's Word, God's Word is there. We must do it!" As he now cries against images, "God's Word, God's Word!" My dear lords, Mr. Everybody is not to be toyed with. Therefore God would have authorities so that there might be order in the world.

If it were really true, and I could believe, that Dr. Karlstadt does not intend murder or rebellion, I would still have to say that he has a rebellious and murderous spirit, like the one at Allstedt, as long as he continues with wanton image breaking and draws the unruly rabble to himself. I well see that he neither strikes nor stabs, but since he carries the murderous weapon and does not put it aside, I do not trust him. He could be waiting for time and place, and then do what I fear. By the murderous weapon I mean the false interpretation and understanding of the law of Moses. Through it the devil comes and the masses are aroused to boldness and arrogance.

You say, however, Oh, he won't be that obstinate. He is willing to be instructed and desist from such things. Who? Dr. Karlstadt? To be sure, he can say the words very well, and blare forth in writings that he wants to be instructed and would listen to a superior. If he's in earnest, I'm happy. But when has he ever yielded or listened? How often has not Philip [Melanchthon] admonished him at Wittenberg that he should not rave so about Moses, images, the mass, and confession? And when I came back and preached[16] against his image breaking and celebration of the mass, why did he not then desist and listen?...

15. The Saale River flows through Orlamünde where Karlstadt had served as pastor in 1523 and 1524.

16. The Eight Sermons of March 1522 (see above, Chap. 2).

17. The incident Luther here recalls is not in the account of the encounter at the Black Bear (see Chap. 3).

Also, at Jena in the inn,[17] when we talked of the matter, and he sought to defend his cause most strongly, he turned to me, snapped his fingers and said, "You are nothing to me." If he doesn't respect me, whom among us will he then respect? Or why should I then continue to admonish? I think he nevertheless considers me one of the most learned at Wittenberg. And yet he tells me to my face that I am nothing to him, and then pretends that he seeks to be instructed.

. . . .

These prophets[18] teach and hold also that they are going to reform Christendom and establish it anew in this manner. They must slaughter all princes and the wicked, so that they become lords on earth and live only among saints. Such and much else I myself have heard from them. Dr. Karlstadt knows also that these are fanatics and murderous spirits and that such calamity has originated with them, which should be warning enough. Yet he does not avoid them. And I am to believe that he would not bring about murder and rebellion? Also when I reproached him about this in Jena,[19] he himself admitted it and moreover defended it, saying, why should he not hold to them in that which they say rightly? Why then does he not also hold to us or to the papists, where we are in the right. Or is nothing right with us, or with the papists? No, against these prophets he can neither preach nor write, but against us there must be preaching, writing, and raging.

. . . .

Yes, why have they themselves shown so little love, and so busily worked against us behind our backs in their hiding place, written against us in several territories,[20] and in the pulpit pulled no one to pieces but the Wittenbergers, and yet they have thus far not shown us our error? Wittenberg has done it, on that the spirit feasts. Otherwise all's well in the world. And this is done under the protection of our princes, yes, under our name and sponsorship. . . .

18. On Müntzer and the Zwickau Prophets see above, p. 40, n. 7. Luther clearly identified Karlstadt with these fanatics (e.g., *WA*, Br 3, 256; *LW* 40, 79).

19. At the Black Bear; see Chap. 3, p. 47.

20. With one exception, the tone of which was moderate, Karlstadt did not directly attack Luther in print until Luther challenged him to do so at Jena (see *ABK-S*, p. 179).

But take care, you evil and wrathful spirits. It is still true that Wittenberg is too big a bite for you, and God may ordain that in swallowing you may choke to death on it. We know Satan, and if sometimes we doze off as men, it will do you no good, for he does not slumber nor sleep, who protects and watches over us [Ps. 121:4]. We commit ourselves to him.

Dr. Karlstadt has brought this trouble and misfortune upon himself, in my opinion, inasmuch as he carries on his enterprise without call while wilfully leaving his own calling. For he has forced himself upon Orlamünde as a wolf. For this reason it was impossible for him to do any good there. He was appointed to Wittenberg on a royally endowed income, as an archdeacon, to preach God's Word, lecture, and dispute. God had sent him there, and he agreed to discharge his responsibilities. He did serve for a time, usefully and with honor, and was liked and cherished. He cannot say it was otherwise. He received more advancement from the elector than many others, until the murderous prophets came and made the man wild and restless, so that he wanted to learn something better and more unusual than God teaches in the Bible.

Then he wantonly left and went to Orlamünde, without the knowledge and consent of either the prince or the university. He drove out the pastor who by order of the prince and university privilege was placed there, and personally took over the parish.[21] What do you think of a stunt like that? Does it contribute to quiet obedience to authority, or to insolent rebellion among the masses? . . . Even if the devil bursts, he will be unable to deny that the princes of Saxony sit as governing authorities ordained by God. The land and the people are subject to them. What kind of a spirit then is this that despises such a divine order, proceeds with head-

21. Luther's account is mistaken. Documents published in 1910 demonstrate that at least as early as 1522, Karlstadt's vicar at Orlamünde failed to meet financial obligations. After the vicar reneged on his first agreement to leave by September 1522, Duke John threatened ducal intervention if the vicar did not leave the Orlamünde pastorate by May 1, 1523. See Johannes Trefftz, "Karlstadt und Glitzsch," *Archiv für Reformationsgeschichte*, 7 (1910), 348–50. Later, on May 26, 1523, the Orlamünde Council and Karlstadt wrote Duke John for permission for Karlstadt to go to Orlamünde as pastor. After correspondence with the elector, Karlstadt moved, believing that he had met the elector's conditions. For the correspondence, see E. Hase, "Karlstadt in Orlamünde," *Mitteilungen der Geschichts—und Altertumsforschende Gesellschaft des Osterlandes*, 4 (1858), 89–93. For a lengthy discussion of all the details, see *ABK-S*, pp. 182–88.

strong violence, treats princely possessions and rights as though they were his own, and doesn't even once recognize the prince or confer with him about it, as though he were a blockhead, and he himself were prince in the land? Should not a good spirit fear God's order a little more, and since the estate, the pastorate, and the land belong to the prince, first humbly beg permission to leave and resign one position, and beg the favor of being installed in another?

. . . .

When, however, he alleges, together with the Orlamünders, that he has been elected by them as their minister,[22] and thus externally called, I answer: To me it doesn't matter that they afterward have elected him. I speak about his first coming. Let him produce letters to show that they at Orlamünde have summoned him from Wittenberg and that he did not himself run over there.[23]

. . . .

I am of the opinion that the land belongs to the princes of Saxony and not to Dr. Karlstadt, who is a guest therein and has nothing. When they take from no one what belongs to him and at the same time, for reasons of their own, no longer want someone in their land, I do not believe they are obligated to say to each one what has actuated them, nor to take the matter to court. For princes must conceal many things and keep them secret. If a landlord did not have the right and the power to ask a guest or a servant to move out, without first giving a reason and settling the matter in court, he would be but a poor landlord imprisoned in his own estate, and the guest would himself be landlord.

. . . .

What think you now? Is it not a fine new spiritual humility? Wearing a felt hat and a gray garb,[24] not wanting to be called Doctor, but Brother Andrew and dear neighbor, as another peasant, subject to the magistrate of Orlamünde and obedient as an ordinary citizen. Thus with self-chosen humility and servility, which God

22. Applying Luther's published assertion that a congregation had a right to call its own pastor, the Orlamünders elected Karlstadt pastor in the spring of 1524 (*ABK-S*, pp. 192–93).

23. See n. 21.

24. See below, pp. 134–36 for Karlstadt's reply.

does not command, he wants to be seen and praised as a remarkable Christian, as though Christian behavior consisted in such external hocus-pocus...

Concerning the Mass

Herewith an answer has been given to several of Dr. Karlstadt's books.[25] We shall now give our attention to the book which has to do with the mass,...[26]

. . . .

The other matter about the elevation[27] of the sacrament is of the same kind. This must also be anti-Christian and papistic. Oh if someone could advise this man to leave both preaching and writing alone and do some other work! He is unfortunately not suited for it. He wants to make new laws and sins and set up new articles of faith. Whether it pleases God or not, he can do nothing else.

Already, at an early date, we have taught Christian liberty from [the writings] of St. Paul. There is to be freedom of choice in everything that God has not clearly taught in the New Testament, for example, in matters pertaining to various foods, beverages, attire, places, persons, and various forms of conduct [Rom. 14:2-6; I Cor. 8:8-10]. We are obligated to do nothing at all for God, except believe and love. Now tell me, where has Christ forbidden us to elevate the sacrament or commanded us to elevate it? Show me one little word, and I will yield. Yet Dr. Karlstadt ventures to burst out and say that it is forbidden by Christ, and considers it a sin as great as the denial of God. He is unable to prove this. Nor is it true. Is it not a woeful, pitiable blindness, so to burden souls with sin and murder them, and make laws where none exist?

Tell me, my brother, what do you think of the spirit who dares command and direct the Christian to do what Christ does

25. See above, p. 95, n. 2.

26. I have omitted the section in which Luther replied to Karlstadt's objection to calling the sacrament a mass. Karlstadt mistakenly claimed that "mass" means sacrifice in Hebrew. He also claimed that the elevation of the host implied the Catholic idea of eucharistic sacrifice.

27. In this section, Luther is attacking Karlstadt's statements against elevation in *Wider die alte und newe papistische Messen* (*St. L.* 20, 2306–13). Karlstadt condemned elevation of the consecrated elements on two grounds: (1) in the Old Testament, the sacrifices were elevated; hence elevation implied that one still accepted the Catholic idea of the sacrifice of the mass; (2) Christ did not elevate the elements at the Last Supper.

not do, yes to do that of which Christ does the opposite? For Christ does not forbid elevation, but leaves it to free choice. This spirit forbids it, and ensnares the conscience due to his own wanton ambition. Is not this to slander Christ? Is not this to deny Christ? Is not this to set oneself in Christ's place and in Christ's name to murder souls, bind consciences, burden with sins, make laws, and, in short, so to deal with souls as if one were their God? All this, and what more there is to be added, he does who makes law and sin where Christ would have freedom and no sin. For this same reason we have shown the pope to be the Antichrist, in that he infringes on such freedom with laws, where Christ would have freedom. And my factious spirit blunders upon the same way. He would make captive what Christ would have free.

However in this respect the profile of the factious spirit differs from that of the pope. They both destroy Christian freedom, and they are both anti-Christian. But the pope does it through commandments, Dr. Karlstadt through prohibitions.

. . . .

Teaching and doing are two things. I say, furthermore, that one should separate teaching and doing as far from each other as heaven from earth. Teaching belongs only to God. He has the right and the power to command, forbid, and be master over the conscience. However, to do and refrain from doing belong to us so that we may keep God's commandment and teaching. Where doing or to refrain from doing is in question, and concerning which God has taught, commanded, and forbidden nothing, there we should permit free choice as God himself has done.

. . . .

Now, dear sirs, we are speaking of minor matters, insofar as the doing is concerned. For what does it mean to elevate the sacrament? But when the teaching is taken into account we are dealing with the most important matters. The factious spirit is too frivolous and meddles all too impudently in this matter. He has such a low regard for teaching and such a high regard for the doing. . . .

However, we thank him kindly for teaching us that Christ did not elevate the sacrament in the Last Supper, although we also already knew this, and almost as well as he. We are talking here about teaching, not doing, and beg him to show us where Christ teaches or forbids elevation. We already know where he refrains from doing it or does not do it. But we are of the opinion that it is not necessary to do or refrain from doing all that Christ has done or refrained from doing. Otherwise we would also have to walk on the sea, and do all the miracles that he has done. Furthermore, we would have to refrain from marriage, abandon temporal authority, forsake field and plow, and all that he has refrained from doing. For that which he would have us do or not do, he has not only done or not done himself, but in addition he has explained in words that command and forbid what we are to do and refrain from doing. For when he says, John 16 [John 13:15]: "I have given you an example, that you also should do as I have done to you," he applies this, not to Lazarus, whom he had raised from the dead, but to the act of footwashing.

Therefore we will admit no example, not even from Christ himself, much less from other saints, for it must also be accompanied by God's Word, which explains to us in what sense we are to follow or not to follow it. We do not consider works and examples adequate, indeed we do not want to follow any example: we want the Word, for the sake of which all works, examples, and miracles occur. For certainly he is sufficiently wise and articulate, and able to anticipate the future so as to indicate in words everything which is commanded or forbidden. Well now, heigh, you factious spirits, rave on as best you can and show us, where has Christ with one tittle forbidden the elevation of the sacrament? Since you still boast and bluster that Christ prohibits it, where is the prohibition?...

And although I had intended also to abolish the elevation, now I will not do it, to defy for a while the fanatic spirit, since he would forbid it and consider it a sin and make us depart from our liberty.[28] . . . This matter of Christian liberty is nothing to joke about.

. . . .

...When one now holds before you how Christ has done it, speak up briskly: Very well, he has done it. Has he also taught and commanded it to be done? Also if one holds before you, this Christ has not done, then speak up briskly: Has he also forbidden it? And if they cannot point to his Word,

28. The elevation of the host was not abolished in Wittenberg until 1542, after the death of Karlstadt (*LW* 40, 134, n. 83).

then say: Put it aside, let it be. That doesn't apply to me. Nor is it an example, it is his work, done for his own part.

. . . .

. . . Dr. Karlstadt does not and cannot teach Moses spiritually, as he reveals sin and physically drives rough and rude people to works. He constructs his own Moses. Thus here he also constructs his own Christ, that we are to follow his works without the Word. But he does not understand how Christ is first of all our salvation, and thereafter his works with the Word are our example. He knows no more about the New Testament than he does about the Old, and yet he would write about the sacrament and such matters, as though there were great need for his absurd and blind art, and, indeed, his folly.

For how is a true understanding of Moses or the law possible, so that the knowledge of sin is taught (Rom. 3 [:20], and rough people are driven to works (Lev. 18 [:4-5]), when one so interprets it that the disorderly populace is to revolt and usurp the office of the temporal authority, and thereby overturn the whole order and meaning of the law? Furthermore, how is it possible for anyone to understand Christ correctly, as he is given to us in faith unto life, and his words and works are given in love as an example, who goes off in another direction and only emphasizes how we, bidden and unforbidden, are to regard Christ's works as a necessary example and are to follow them? There faith and love together with the whole gospel must perish. And that is why they speak so scornfully of the doctrine of faith and love,[29] as even Dr. Karlstadt himself threw it in my face in Jena,[30] just as if they knew something much higher and better. Yet they do not speak out plainly, nor do they want to bring it out into the open. Even when taken by itself this behavior shows that the devil speaks through them, since they ridicule the doctrine of faith and love, that is, Christ himself with his gospel.

. . . .

But it is the same fiddle upon which he always fiddles, namely, that the external appearance is the main thing, according to which everything that the heart, mouth, pen, and hand confesses is to be

29. See above, pp. 54–55, for Karlstadt's view that talk of brotherly love was an excuse for protecting images. See also below, pp. 128–29, where Karlstadt denies that he has neglected his "faith."

30. For the incident at Jena, see above, p. 42.

regarded and judged. Therefore it does not help that we believe with the heart, confess with the mouth, testify with the pen, and demonstrate with deeds that we do not regard the sacrament as a sacrifice, though we still elevate it. The elevation is so important and by itself counts for so much, that it outweighs and condemns everything else. Is this not a vexatious spirit, who so juggles with external appearance against the truth in the spirit? If only the elevation were permitted to remain an external matter....

. . . .

Dr. Karlstadt has fallen from the kingdom of Christ and has suffered shipwreck with respect to faith. Therefore he wants to get us out of the kingdom right into works and simply make Galatians of us also.

. . . .

...Whoever insists that the sacrament may not be elevated, as a matter of necessity is a Gentile. In doing this Dr. Karlstadt sets up a law compelling the conscience, which only God has a right to do. But whoever elevates the sacrament with such a conscience and the intention of making it an offering is one who sacrifices, and a papist. For where such a conscience exists, there one sacrifices, even if one never elevated the sacrament or even sank it into a deep well. Where, however, such a conscience does not exist, there one does not sacrifice, even if one raised it above the heavens and the whole world shouted: Sacrifice, sacrifice! For everything depends on the conscience. Of this the fanatic spirit knows nothing, or does not want to know anything.

I imagine the reading of this treatise will annoy many, since it deals with such charlatanry. But how can I avoid it? This mad spirit drives me to it. Yet, as I said above, we have some fruit from it in that we defend and understand more clearly our Christian freedom. We also recognize this false spirit for what he is and see how he is blind and stupid in all things. Everyone may therefore govern himself accordingly. For since he does not understand such trifling [external] things, but so magnifies them as to usurp the office of God, making laws, sin, and matters of conscience where none exist, destroying Christian liberty, and enticing consciences away from an understanding of grace to external works and appearance, so that Christ is denied, his kingdom destroyed, and the gospel reviled—who then can hope that he will ever be able to write or teach anything that is good? For certainly one can prove from this matter that the spirit of Christ is lacking. It must be the devil that is there, and so he is. Let each one govern himself accordingly.

. . . .

PART II

Our controversy[31] has no doubt given great joy to the papists and inspired among them the hope that our cause would thereby suffer defeat. So be it, let them boast and exalt over us. Often and repeatedly I have said that if our cause is of God no one will be able to suppress it. If it is not of God, I will not be able to support it whatever someone else does. I can lose nothing by it for I have won nothing. But this I know that no one but God himself can take it from me. However much I regret this vexation, I am glad that the devil now reveals himself and his shamefulness through these heavenly prophets. They have long grumbled to themselves and would not even have come out into the open unless I had lured them out through a gulden.[32] This I believe, by God's grace, to be a good investment which I do not regret.

. . . .

Out of his great mercy God has again given us the pure gospel, the noble and precious treasure of our salvation. This gift evokes faith and a good conscience in the inner man, as is promised in Isa. 55 [:1], that his Word will not go forth in vain, and Rom. 10 [:17], that "faith comes through preaching." The devil hates this gospel and will not tolerate it. Since he has not succeeded hitherto in opposing it with power of sword, he now, as indeed always, seeks victory by deceit and false prophets. I ask you, Christian reader, to observe carefully. If God wills I will help you to discern the devil in these prophets so that you can yourself deal with him. It is for your good, not mine, that I write. Follow me thus:

Now when God sends forth his holy gospel he deals with us in a twofold manner, first outwardly, then inwardly. Outwardly he deals with us through the oral word of the gospel and through

31. In Part II of this work, Luther is responding primarily to Karlstadt's *Dialogus* (see above, p. 95, n. 2).

32. A reference to the confrontation at Jena; see above, pp. 47–48.

material signs, that is, baptism and the sacrament of the altar. Inwardly he deals with us through the Holy Spirit, faith, and other gifts. But whatever their measure or order the outward factors should and must precede. The inward experience follows and is effected by the outward. God has determined to give the inward to no one except through the outward. For he wants to give no one the Spirit or faith outside of the outward Word and sign instituted by him, as he says in Luke 16 [:29], "Let them hear Moses and the prophets." Accordingly Paul can call baptism a "washing of regeneration" wherein God "richly pours out the Holy Spirit" [Tit. 3:5]. And the oral gospel "is the power of God for salvation to every one who has faith" (Rom. 1 [:16]).

Observe carefully, my brother, this order, for everything depends on it. However cleverly this factious spirit makes believe that he regards highly the Word and Spirit of God and declaims passionately about love and zeal for the truth and righteousness of God, he nevertheless has as his purpose to reverse this order. His insolence leads him to set up a contrary order and, as we have said, seeks to subordinate God's outward order to an inner spiritual one. Casting this order to the wind with ridicule and scorn, he wants to get to the Spirit first. Will a handful of water, he says, make me clean from sin? The Spirit, the Spirit, the Spirit, must do this inwardly. Can bread and wine profit me? Will breathing over the bread bring Christ in the sacrament? No, no, one must eat the flesh of Christ spiritually. The Wittenbergers are ignorant of this. They make faith depend on the letter. Whoever does not know the devil might be misled by these many splendid words to think that five holy spirits were in the possession of Karlstadt and his followers.

But should you ask how one gains access to this same lofty spirit they do not refer you to the outward gospel but to some imaginary realm, saying: Remain in "self-abstraction"[33] where I now am and you will have the same experience. A heavenly voice will come, and God himself will speak to you. If you inquire further as to the nature of this "self-abstraction," you will find that they know as much about it as Dr. Karlstadt knows of Greek and Hebrew. Do you not see here the devil, the enemy of God's order? With all his mouthing of the words, "Spirit, Spirit, Spirit," he tears down the bridge, the path, the way, the ladder, and all the means

33. One of the seven stages in the mystic apprehension of God.

by which the Spirit might come to you.[34] Instead of the outward order of God in the material sign of baptism and the oral proclamation of the Word of God he wants to teach you, not how the Spirit comes to you but how you come to the Spirit. They would have you learn how to journey on the clouds and ride on the wind. They do not tell you how or when, whither or what, but you are to experience what they do.

. . . .

They pay no attention to God's design of inward things, such as faith. They approach and force all external words and Scriptures belonging to the inward life of faith into new forms of putting to death the old Adam. They invent such things as "turning from the material," "concentration," "adoration," "self-abstraction,"[35] and other such foolishness which has not an inkling of foundation in Scripture. My Karlstadt plunges in like a sow to devour pearls, and like a dog tearing holy things to pieces [Matt. 7:6]. What Christ has said and referred to the inner life of faith, this man applies to outward, self-contrived works, even to the point of making the Lord's Supper and the recognition and remembrance of Christ a human work, whereby we in like manner, in "passionate ardor" and (as they stupidly put it) with "outstretched desire," put ourselves to death. By throwing up a smoke screen, he obscures the clear words of Christ, "My blood poured out for you for the forgiveness of sins," etc. [Matt. 26:28; Mark 14:24; Luke 22:20]. Their meaning undoubtedly is grasped, received, and retained only by faith, and by no kind of work. This will become clearer as we proceed.

Enough has been said so that you may know that it is of the nature of this spirit to press for a way the reverse of that ordered by God. That which God has made a matter of inward faith and spirit they convert into a human work. But what God has ordained as an outward word and sign and work they convert into an inner spirit. They place the mortification of the flesh prior to faith,[36] even prior to the Word. In devil's fashion they go out where God

34. This is a misunderstanding of Karlstadt's theology. Karlstadt continued to believe, with Augustine, that the external word was necessary in the mediation of grace but was insufficient without the activity of the Holy Spirit. See below, pp. 127–34 and the many quotations in *ABK*-S, pp. 238–46.

35. For a discussion of Karlstadt's use of mystical terminology, see ibid. pp. 206–36, 301–2.

36. See Karlstadt's reply below, p. 128.

would enter and enter where he goes out. It ought surprise no one that I call him a devil. For I am not thinking of Dr. Karlstadt or concerned about him. I am thinking of him by whom he is possessed and for whom he speaks, as St. Paul says, "For we are not contending against flesh and blood—but against the spiritual hosts of wickedness in the heavenly places" [Eph. 6:12].

So, my brother, cling firmly to the order of God. According to it the putting to death of the old man, wherein we follow the example of Christ, as Peter says [I Pet. 2:21], does not come first, as this devil urges, but comes last. No one can mortify the flesh, bear the cross, and follow the example of Christ before he is a Christian and has Christ through faith in his heart as an eternal treasure. You don't put the old nature to death, as these prophets do, through works, but through the hearing of the gospel.[37]

. . . .

. . . We have the verse in I Cor. 11 [:27], "Whoever eats the bread or drinks the cup of the Lord in an unworthy manner will be guilty of profaning the body and blood of the Lord." Here again the sectarian spirit goes off and makes into spiritual that which St. Paul affirms is body, and attributes unworthy eating to those who do not have a right understanding of Christ and remembrance of his body.[38] If again you ask, where is this written? What is the basis for it? Where is the text? He will show his anger and give no other evidence than that he has been burned by such verses, and would rather forestall them as impertinent, just as if I would seek to persuade someone who waved a naked sword over me to believe that it was a straw, so that he would not strike me.

. . . .

Now the nature and character of the sentence requires us to interpret it to mean that whoever eats unworthily is guilty in regard

37. In the thirty-three pages here omitted, Luther first argues against Karlstadt's exegetical reasons for denying the Real Presence and then develops an exegetical basis for his own eucharistic doctrine. At the point where we now pick up his argument he is seeking to show that Karlstadt "makes everything spiritual and inward which God has determined should be outward and bodily; on the other hand he makes that outward and bodily which God wills should be inward and spiritual" (*LW* 40, 178–79). For the kind of statement in Karlstadt which Luther is attacking, see above, pp. 76–87.

38. See Karlstadt's exegesis of this verse, above, pp. 83–87.

to what he eats. Therefore, it is not enough for Dr. Karlstadt to say "no" and insert an interpolation. Since the text here is clear, and the nature and meaning of the language used affirm that whoever eats this bread unworthily is guilty of profaning the body of the Lord because the body of the Lord is eaten in the bread, and sin is committed in the eating and drinking, therefore he would have to bring forward convincing verses and text, if we were to believe him. For the text forcefully compels the interpretation that sin is committed in the eating and drinking, as it says, "Whoever eats and drinks unworthily," and yet claims that the same sin has to do with the body and blood of the Lord. This strongly indicates that it is in the eating of the body and drinking of the blood of Christ that the unworthy one has offended and therein committed evil.

For the unworthy remembrance of the Lord is a separate sin other than the unworthy eating, and St. Paul says nothing of it in this place. All the words in the entire chapter where he condemns the unworthy eating indicate that the sin consists wholly in eating and drinking. St. Paul terrifies them lest they think it is merely bread or wine which they eat and drink, thereby becoming unworthy, when it is the body and blood of Christ, which makes them guilty of such unworthy eating. Such, I said, is the natural meaning, and one can see that Dr. Karlstadt's mocking objections are altogether artificial, forced, and obstinate, on which no conscience or faith can rely.

It is not sound reasoning arbitrarily to associate the sin which St. Paul attributes to eating with remembrance of Christ, of which Paul does not speak.

. . . .

In brief, this is the spirit of whom I have already said that he makes inward whatever God makes outward. So he has to do here. The guilt which Paul places in the bodily eating and drinking he makes an inner one, in a spiritual eating and drinking. From the fact that he fumes that those unworthily eat and drink who do not inwardly acknowledge the body of Christ nor rightly hold him in remembrance, we can understand that he transfers the eating and drinking into the spirit, though Paul considers it an outward act. For spiritual eating is the right recognition and remembrance of the body of Christ. Do you not again become aware of this devil with all his spirituality, though he has no basis, Scripture, argument, or other evidence than what he spins from his own brain? ... St. Paul writes in the same chapter, "Let a man examine himself, and so eat of the bread and drink of the cup. For anyone who eats and drinks without discerning the body eats and drinks judgment upon himself" [I Cor. 11:28-29] ... Look a little closer with us on the text. You say that the discerning belongs to the remembrance. But Paul says it applies to the eating and drinking. For he does not say, "Who unworthily holds the Lord in remembrance merits judgment, since he does not discern the body of the Lord." But he speaks thus, "Who eats and drinks unworthily, he eats and drinks judgment to himself, for he does not discern the body of the Lord." Do you hear that, Peter?[39] In an unworthy eating and drinking this discerning is lacking, therefore judgment is the penalty. Is that not clear enough? Does not the text demand this?

. . . .

So we conclude that this discerning *is* to take place in the eating and drinking, as above; guilt and sin occur in relation to the body of the Lord. Who, thus, eats and drinks unworthily eats unto his judgment. Why? Because, Paul says, he does not discern the body of Christ. Now tell me, how does one discern the body of the Lord in eating and drinking? The Greek word, *diakrinein,* in Latin, *discernere,* means to make a distinction, and not to think of one thing like the other, but to consider the one thing nobler, better, more precious than the other. St. Paul means that whoever eats and drinks unworthily, fittingly deserves judgment or severe punishment, because with his unworthy eating and drinking he does not distinguish, does not discern, the body of Christ, but thinks of and treats the bread and wine of the Lord as if it were merely bread and wine, though it is the body and blood of the Lord. For if he seriously thought of it as the body of the Lord, he would not act so carelessly, as if it were ordinary bread, but would eat with fear, humility, and reverence. He ought of course have a sense of awe before the body of the Lord.

. . . .

39. Peter Rültz was one of Karlstadt's mouthpieces in the eucharistic dialogue which Luther is attacking.

But one ought not blame Dr. Karlstadt. As I have said, since his spirit is bent on making spiritual what God wants to be bodily, he has to treat the discernment in this way, making recognition and remembrance a spiritual discernment, inward in the spirit, when God intends a bodily discernment, between bread and the body of Christ. Should one require him to show the basis and reason for his position, or to present a compelling argument on the basis of the text? Brother, do not bewilder him with such a request. Don't you see that he has other things to do? It is enough that such a man says it. If you don't believe him, believe his gray peasant coat and felt hat, in which, as you ought to know, the Holy Spirit must be.

. . . .

. . . I have often asserted that the ultimate goal of the devil is to do away with the entire sacrament and all outward ordinances of God. Then as these prophets teach, all that would count would be for the heart to stare inwardly at the spirit.

. . . .

But suppose your knowledge and remembrance of Christ were this pure passion, pure heart, pure ardor, pure fire, before which also the sectarian spirits were to melt away and were to blow up their spirituality with words which are a thousand times more high-sounding, what then? What would be gained? Nothing except new monks and hypocrites who would with greater devotion and earnestness stand before the bread and wine (if everything went well), as hitherto the sensitive consciences have stood before the sacrament. Indeed as great a concern and anxiety would manifest itself about this knowledge and remembrance as hitherto has been felt for the worthy reception of the body of Christ. For the acknowledgment which they advocate accomplishes nothing. Even the devil knows full well and recognizes that the body of Christ is given for us, yet this does not help him.

The knowledge, however, does help if I do not doubt, but in true faith hold firmly that the body and blood of Christ are given for me, for me, for me (I repeat), in order to take away my sins, as the word in the sacrament affirms, "This is the body, given for you." This knowledge produces joyful, free, and assured consciences. This is the meaning in Isa. 53 [:11], "By his knowledge he will make many to be accounted righteous." This teaching is as hostile as death to Dr. Karlstadt's spirit, and in his desire to eradicate it he makes a great ado about "passionate, heartfelt, earnest knowledge of the body of Christ,"[40] as if he were much in earnest, yet he really stifles it. He thinks one does not see that out of the word of Christ he makes a pure commandment and law which accomplish nothing more than to tell and bid us to remember and acknowledge him. Furthermore, he makes this acknowledgment nothing else than a work that we do, while we receive nothing else than bread and wine. But more of this later.

. . . .

From this you can grasp that Dr. Karlstadt's theology has not gotten beyond teaching how we are to imitate Christ, making of Christ only an example and lawgiver.[41] From this only works can be learned. He does not know and teach Christ as our treasure and the gift of God, from which faith follows, and which is the highest of doctrines. All this he wants to dress up and obscure with these words: passionate knowledge, ardent remembrance, and the like. He descends from faith to works in a manner that I long ago observed would lead his teaching and skill to a point where he would affirm that the free will plays a part in the things of God and in good works.

Further, the mad spirit is so ignorant of Scripture that he interprets the word "remembrance," where Christ says, "This do in remembrance of me," only in the manner of the sophists [scholastic teachers] to mean, the inner thoughts of the heart, as one would think of anyone. For this spirit must be inward, and make inward and spiritual what God wants to be outward, so that nothing will be external. But it is still more mischievous and malicious, that he gives such remembrance the power to justify, as faith does. The proof he gives is, he says, that it is written, "That they have done this in remembrance of me." What think you? It is written, "They have done it in remembrance of me." Therefore such remembrance justifies. There you comprehend how well Dr.

40. For example see above, pp. 76–87, esp. pp. 79–80.

41. This is clearly wrong. For many quotations demonstrating that Christ's atoning work on the cross and his sanctifying indwelling of the believer in addition to his role as example were central to Karlstadt's theology, see *ABK*-S, pp. 254–59; see also Chap. 5 above.

Karlstadt understands the Lord's Supper, his remembrance, and justification, namely, that the devil shows only ridicule and scorn in these matters.

You should, however, know and hold that this remembrance of Christ is an outward remembrance, as one can speak of remembering anyone. This is the way the Scriptures speak of it, for example, in Psalm 15 [Ps. 16:4]: "I will not take their names upon my lips"; Psalm 10 [Ps. 9:6]: "The very memory of them is perished"; Psalm 72 [Ps. 83:4] "Let the name of Israel be remembered no more"; Psalm 111 [Ps. 112:1]: "The righteous will be remembered for ever." By the words, "This do in remembrance of me," Christ meant what Paul meant by his words, "Proclaim the death of the Lord," etc. [I Cor. 11:26]. Christ wants us to make him known when we receive the sacrament and proclaim the gospel, so as to confirm faith. He does not want us to sit and indulge in such fancies and make out of such a remembrance a good work, as Dr. Karlstadt dreams. Would that these prophets had put in more time in study before they published books.

From this you know well that such remembrance does not justify, but that they must first be justified who would preach, proclaim, and practice the outward remembrance of Christ, as it is written in Rom. 10 [:10], "For man believes with his heart and so is justified, and he confesses with his lips and so is saved." The righteousness which Dr. Karlstadt produces out of remembrance, however, avails nothing and you should beware of it. He lies to you and deceives you. For he does not make such knowledge spiritual as it ought to be. For Isaiah [Isa. 53:11] speaks of a spirit and of a spiritual knowledge which the Holy Spirit works in us, not we ourselves. I know and am convinced beyond doubt that this is the same as, Christ is given for me. But Dr. Karlstadt makes of it a human, carnal devotion and a passionate, ardent work in the heart, though not higher than the knowledge and recognition that Christ is given for us, which the devil and the hypocrites also know. He can teach knowledge, but not the use of knowledge. He spews out much about knowledge, but does not develop or rightly apply it, but permits it to remain a mere human work. That is to make it a carnal instead of a spiritual knowledge. For his spirit will not tolerate anything less than making carnal what is spiritual.

. . . .

Frau Hulda's fifth attempt is directed especially toward the Luther[42] who has taught that when a person has a conscience troubled by sin he should go to the sacrament and there obtain comfort and the forgiveness of sins. Here Peter Rültz[43] is first of all a fine fellow and speaks boldly: "O you false prophets, you promise the kingdom of God to the people for a piece of bread. I know that you do not improve the bread by your secret breathing and whispering, why then do you say that sins can be forgiven when you have blown upon it? Why do you not just as well take a handful of barley, etc., and eat it in God's name, so that you may be free from your sins?"[44] Here I must speak with Dr. Karlstadt himself.

. . . .

Tell me, first, spirit of lies, when have we ever taught that a piece of bread forgives sins?. . .

Secondly, tell me when we whisper or breathe upon the bread? Ah, now, show me! And where have we ever taught that our whispering and breathing have improved the bread? Ah, now, why don't you answer? All right, I will take an oath. If Dr. Karlstadt believes there is any God in heaven or on earth, may Christ my Lord never more be merciful and gracious to me. I know that is a serious oath. My reason for it is that Dr. Karlstadt knows that we do not breathe or whisper over the bread, but do speak the divine, almighty, heavenly, and holy words which Christ himself spoke at the supper with his holy lips and commanded us to speak.

. . . .

Even if I followed the Karlstadtian teaching and preached the remembrance and knowledge of Christ with such passion and seriousness that I sweated blood and became feverish, it would be of no avail and all in vain. For it would be pure work and commandment, but no gift or Word of God offered and given to me in

42. Earlier, Luther had referred to "natural reason" as "Frau Hulda" whom he considered a seductive "devil's prostitute" in matters of faith (*LW* 40, 174–75). Luther's previous four points, treated under the subhead "Concerning Frau Hulda, Dr. Karlstadt's Shrewd Reason, in this Sacrament," have been omitted except for a portion of point three.

43. See n. 39 above.

44. Luther partly quotes from and partly paraphrases—accurately—Karlstadt's *Dialogus*; Hertzsch 2, 29.

the body and blood of Christ. It would be as if I had a chest full of gold and great treasure buried or preserved in a certain place. I might think myself to death and experience all desire, great passion, and ardor in such knowledge and remembrance of the treasure until I became ill. But what benefit would all this be to me if this treasure were not opened, given, and brought to me and placed in my keeping? It would mean truly to love, but not to enjoy.

. . . .

So that our readers may the better perceive our teaching I shall clearly and broadly describe it. We treat of the forgiveness of sins in two ways. First, how it is achieved and won. Second, how it is distributed and given to us. Christ has achieved it on the cross, it is true. But he has not distributed or given it on the cross. He has not won it in the supper or sacrament. There he has distributed and given it through the Word, as also in the gospel, where it is preached. He has won it once for all on the cross. But the distribution takes place continuously, before and after, from the beginning to the end of the world. For inasmuch as he had determined once to achieve it, it made no difference to him whether he distributed it before or after, through his Word, as can easily be proved from Scripture. But now there is neither need nor time to do so.

If now I seek the forgiveness of sins, I do not run to the cross, for I will not find it given there. Nor must I hold to the suffering of Christ, as Dr. Karlstadt trifles, in knowledge or remembrance, for I will not find it there either. But I will find in the sacrament or gospel the word which distributes, presents, offers, and gives to me that forgiveness which was won on the cross. Therefore, Luther has rightly taught that whoever has a bad conscience from his sins should go to the sacrament and obtain comfort, not because of the bread and wine, not because of the body and blood of Christ, but because of the word which in the sacrament offers, presents, and gives the body and blood of Christ, given and shed for me. Is that not clear enough?

Yet this mad spirit has attacked us and said, O you false prophets, you have no word in the sacrament which presents or gives you the forgiveness of sins. I repeat, he should have attacked the word in the sacrament on which we stand, defiantly and persistently, and should have proved that we do not have it there. Then he would have been a valiant knight. Even if only bread and wine were there present, as they claim, as long as the word, "Take, eat, this is my body given for you," etc., is there, the forgiveness of sins, on account of this word, would be in the sacrament. Just as in the case of baptism we confess that only water is present, but since the Word of God, which forgives sin, is connected with it, we readily say with St. Paul, that baptism is a bath of regeneration and renewal. Everything depends on the Word.

There you have, my reader, Dr. Karlstadt's devil and can see how he has proposed to destroy the external Word of God, which also he does not regard or consider or designate as anything more than a whisper, breath, or blowing. Also, you can see how he has wanted to abolish the sacrament altogether, both bodily and spiritually, denying the bodily presence of the body and blood of Christ and the spiritual presence of the forgiveness of sins, so that neither the sacrament nor its fruits remain. And in place of a divine ordinance and word he has wanted to institute his own fancied remembrance and knowledge. But he lacked the necessary skill. Now you know how to judge him.

. . . .

In closing, I want to warn everyone truly and fraternally to beware of Dr. Karlstadt and his prophets, for two reasons. First, because they run about and teach, without a call.[45] . . .

The second reason is that these prophets avoid, run away from, and are silent about the main points of Christian doctrine.[46] For in no place do they teach how we are to become free from our sins, obtain a good conscience, and win a peaceful and joyful heart before God. This is what really counts. This is a true sign that their spirit is of the devil, who can use unusual new words to excite, terrify, and mislead consciences. But their spirit cannot give quietness or peace, but goes on and teaches special works in which they are to exercise and discipline themselves. They have no idea how a good conscience can be gained or ought to be constituted.

45. See above, p. 44, n. 18, and p. 106, n. 21.

46. Karlstadt replies to the accusation in his *Review of Some of the Chief Articles of Christian Doctrine* (below, pp. 127–38.

For they have not felt or ever recognized it. How can they know or feel it, when they come and teach of themselves, without a call. No good can come in this way.

The grace of God be with us all. Amen.

7
Theological Rebuttal: Karlstadt's *Review of Some of the Chief Articles of Christian Doctrine*

After his expulsion from Saxony Karlstadt traveled from one city to another looking for a place where he could earn a living. Late in 1524 he arrived in Rothenburg on the Tauber, a city destined soon to become a focal point of revolutionary activity in the Peasants' Revolt. Because of pressure from the prince, the city council ordered Karlstadt to leave in January, but he soon returned secretly and lived in hiding in Rothenburg since he could find nowhere else to go.

While here, Luther's *Against the Heavenly Prophets* came to his attention on February 27, 1525. Furious, Karlstadt threatened to write fifteen books against Luther! Of the three he quickly wrote in the next month or two, *A Review of Some of the Chief Articles of Christian Doctrine* is the most important. It is his most comprehensive reply to Luther's *Against the Heavenly Prophets.* Karlstadt explains his understanding of the role of the external Word, insists that his own conception of Christian liberty is as good as Luther's, and stresses the importance of both forgiveness and the life of obedience.

Interesting too is Karlstadt's vigorous identification with the common person. Unlike Luther whose mistrust of "Mr. Everyman" is reflected in his aside in *Against the Heavenly Prophets* that the "crude masses" must be compelled by the sword and the law "much in the manner in which we control wild animals with chains and pens" (above, p. 97), Karlstadt speak highly of the peasants and seeks to identify with their simple life and manual labor.

For the background, see *ABK*-B 2, 279ff. For Karlstadt's theology at this time, see Kriechbaum and *ABK*-S, pp. 202–303. The following excerpts are translated from the reprint of the original edition in Hertzsch 2, 59–104.

A Review of Some of the Chief Articles of Christian Doctrine in which Dr. Luther Brings Andreas Karlstadt under Suspicion through False Accusation and Calumny 1525

Andreas [61] Karlstadt expelled without a trial because of the truth,[1] elected and called to the pure proclamation of the cross of Christ by God the Father, to the brethren on the Saale[2] and to those who seek or eagerly want to seek God in the right way.

. . . .

If [62] I am summoned and tried, I want to demonstrate by my books and by oral confession that Dr. Luther has done me great and intolerable violence. And I defy him to dare to come with me before a Christian congregation and allow them to hear a review of my innocence there.

Do I not know that God's law is spiritual, righteous, holy, and good?[3] [Do I not know] that it makes the inward man spiritual, righteous, holy, and good when God writes and imprints his law on the heart [and] when God's Spirit leads [63] into the truth and speaks into the heart what the external voice cries into the ears so that sin is then rightly understood, comprehended, and fled as being evil?[4] The genuine revelation of sin is of the Spirit, who has given the external, and not of the letter. . . . For he who understands the letter of the law without the revelation of the Spirit does not become hateful toward and an enemy of evil (Rom. 6 [:15]; I Cor. 15 [:56]). Rather he increases in evil through the law. Therefore to know sin

1. See above, p. 102, n. 11.
2. See above, p. 104, n. 15.
3. See Luther's charge that the "prophets" do not understand the spiritual preaching of the law, above, p. 96).
4. There are marginal references here to John 16 [:7–15]; Jer. 31 [:31–34]; Rom. 7 [:7ff.]; 8 [:1–8]. Karlstadt's argument here is very reminiscent of his early Augustinianism of 1517 (*ABK*-S, pp. 25–29). Karlstadt gave extended theological attention to the role of the law (see ibid., 108–22, 238ff., 277ff.).

as it is pertains to the grace of God through Christ. And grace alone takes men away from sin and from the power and influence of the letter of the law which truly kills. For when it is understood by one's own reason God's law reveals sin in such a way that the knower becomes much worse than he was before; desire becomes sin for the first time and becomes anger against God's righteousness and makes sin a thousand times more serious. Therefore there is a distinction between the revelation of evil which the Spirit of Christ bestows and the revelation of sin which the flesh acquires by its own powers. The external revelation of sin through the law fires the sinner with desire and anger and strengthens sin. The inner revelation through the grace of Christ breaks desire, quenches anger, and destroys sin.

. . . .

For [66] the sake of poor Christians, I must boast and confess that I have written about the mortification of the flesh with this difference, that is, without bias, and have extracted the true kernel from the Gospels, the apostles' books, Moses, and the prophets. Often, I accuse Christendom because many preachers do not proclaim the mortification of our life sufficiently.[5] I also point out that some mortification precedes faith, some—and that the best—comes with faith, and some follows.[6]

. . . .

It [69] means nothing that Luther alleges that the chief articles are ignored and forgotten when we do battle over the other, aforesaid articles [i.e., the sacrament, images, etc.]. For there were and also still are other preachers and writers who preach and write while we deal with the other points. Even if Dr. Luther and I slept, Dr. Luther need not worry, for the world does not depend on us. So much for the first point. Second [70], Dr. Luther should know that we cannot handle such issues properly unless we also deal with some, indeed many, articles which he calls chief matters. For how can I demonstrate that the sacrament or the chimerical faith in the sacrament and in the sacramental word cannot forgive any

5. Karlstadt understood himself to be developing a theology which corrected what he considered Luther's one-sided emphasis on *sola fide* and forgiveness of sins and Luther's consequent neglect of mortification of the flesh, regeneration, and good works. His Orlamünde theology stressed regeneration (ibid., pp. 212ff.). See also below, pp. 131, 133–34, 136–38.

6. See Luther's comment on p. 115 above.

sin [and] cannot strengthen the conscience if I do not demonstrate this through the correct faith in Christ the crucified, and through God's Word. How can I suppress faith through this treatment in which I point out, praise, and uphold the pure faith? If I order the removal of that which suppresses true faith, do I then suppress or obscure faith (if I as a poor earthly vessel can do otherwise)? It is the same with the treatment of baptism. He who refuses baptism to those who do not believe and denies baptism until they have become believers furthers the chief article of the faith and does not suppress it.[7]

. . . .

The [74] Following Deals with the Chief Articles

Luther says further: "I will here briefly recount the chief articles of the Christian faith to which everyone is above all things to pay attention and hold fast."[8]

KARLSTADT: Therefore I will truly be on the alert industriously and assiduously to see what the great mountain of Israel will bring forth. Only I fear that he has conceived an elephant and will give birth to a mouse.

DR. LUTHER: "The first is the law of God which is to be preached so that one thereby reveals and teaches how to recognize sin (Rom. 3 [:20]; 7 [:7])."[9]

KARLSTADT: I hoped that Dr. Luther would dig the true kernel of the whole law out of the nut and bring forth the complete spiritual content of the law—that is, what it can do, how far its power stretches and extends. And I waited eagerly for Dr. Luther's offspring. But I see that he broke off only one line of St. Paul's doctrine and did not completely exhibit the content of Paul. . . .

Certainly [75] the law says that we do not understand sin through the law. . . Neither preaching, proclamation of the law,

7. This comment and the brief comment on p. 133 below are among the few surviving comments of Karlstadt's on baptism from this period. Karlstadt's book on baptism was confiscated and destroyed at Basle in 1524. Calvin A. Pater has recently shown that Karlstadt's baptismal tract significantly influenced Anabaptism. See Calvin A. Pater, "Andreas Bodenstein von Karlstadt as the Intellectual Founder of Anabaptism" (Ph.D. dissertation, Harvard University, 1977).

8. Karlstadt begins a lengthy response to Luther's summary (in *Against the Heavenly Prophets*) of the chief articles of Christian faith. See above, p. 96.

9. See above, p. 96.

lash, nor anything else helps unless God sends into the heart of the godless his Spirit who shows him the horror of his evil and causes sin itself to begin to displease him. Man may preach whatever he likes, but the law cannot reveal the idea and understanding of a single sin in the way the revelation should be, that is, with hatred and horror for evil. For that belongs solely to the Spirit of God. Indeed, if the law could insert [*eintrucken*] or pour in (that means reveal according to Christ's way of speaking)[10] the understanding of sin, then the law would be a god.

. . . .

Now [77] when Dr. Luther writes that it should be preached that one reveals and teaches how to recognize sin through the law, he writes an incomplete statement on which one should not build, before the correct and necessary understanding (which is not established in Dr. Luther's chief article) is brought to it. For if Dr. Luther says that the law reveals sin, I can say otherwise with many passages and truly say that the law cannot reveal sin. Paul also wants to say and teaches that, and it is exactly contrary to Dr. Luther's chief article. The law does not reveal sin any more than Scripture reveals Christ—that is, as a witness. Thus I leave the law and go to the Spirit of God; I do not consider the law above all things, as Dr. Luther's devilish doctrine alleges. Nor do I remain with the law, but rather go to him to whom the law points (John 5 [:46]. As Paul says: "The law is a schoolmaster leading to Christ" (Gal. 3 [:24]).

. . . .

Concerning [85] the Second Chief Article

DR. LUTHER: "When sin is recognized and the law is so preached," faith follows.[11]

KARLSTADT: I [86] have written so much about this article in my new booklet[12] that each person can well perceive Dr. Luther's

10. Karlstadt often spoke of the Spirit's activity in the communication of grace in terms of a "revelation," or an "insertion" (*eintrucken*) of the knowledge of God. One misunderstands Karlstadt if one supposes that these passages refer to a spiritualist claim to special, direct revelation of theological truth. (See *ABK-S*, pp. 243–44).

11. See above, p. 96.

12. *Wie sich der gelaub und unglaub* . . . (printed in the fall of 1524 with the eucharistic tracts) is entirely devoted to the subject of "faith." There is no modern reprint.

spirit, and perceive how honest and truthful he is when he writes: "You do not find these two points in these prophets, nor do they know them."[13] But is not this article contained in such a saying as, "Christ has shed his blood for the forgiveness of our sins, Christ has redeemed us, that is, obtained forgiveness of sins"? The wrangling spirit, however, cannot write four lines without lies. (I must not erupt from time to time with irrational words.) For with that kind of invective, Dr. Luther writes that I do not know Christ.[14] Therefore I say that if Dr. Luther writes or says that, he lies as a devilish son of Belial who is neither worthy of honor nor loves God's honor and praise, nor can tolerate the fact that the passion of Christ is known and praised.

It is true that sin should be quickly condemned and established as meriting the wrath of God. And the grace of the cross should be preached so that the sinner who is cast down may treasure Christ's grace all the more highly and hurry and run after it so much more.

The whole gospel of Christ, however, does not consist only of the proclamation of Christ's grace which is shown to be the forgiveness of sins.[15] Rather it [the gospel] is richer. For there are innumerable goods and treasures in Christ, all of which Christ has acquired for us and wants to communicate to us if we believe in him (Eph. 3 [:8, 17ff.]; Tit. 2). What does Dr. Luther think is written in Hebrews about the new testament [e.g., Heb. 7:22; 8:6]? Does not Paul write to the Ephesians about other treasures in addition to the forgiveness of sins? Is it not Good News that all of us together have received of the fullness of Christ (John 1 [:16])? Where does the gospel remain apart from the Spirit of Christ? Where are the rich gifts of the Messiah about which Isaiah writes? Is not the fact that Christ has given the power to become sons of God to all who receive him a special part of the gospel? Or that Christ is the end and perfection of the law? . . .

It [87] is not enough that [the Christian man] knows only how Christ redeemed him by the forgiveness of sins; rather he must know that he must obtain from God through Christ the whole kingdom of all treasures. Dr. Luther does not point that out. Rather,

13. See above, p. 96.
14. See above, p. 120.
15. See n. 5 above.

he presents one line as if the whole gospel of Christ consisted of that one line and as if no one should desire to be taught further by God about the things such as grace, truth, wisdom, strength, and similar treasures which are deposited in Christ so that they flow into us through Christ. These treasures of Christ are written about so that we believe and are saved.

DR. LUTHER: "Christ himself teaches these two articles in such an order at the end of Luke [24:47]: 'One must preach repentance and the forgiveness of sins in his name.' "[16]

KARLSTADT: This text adduced here does not require that one must preach the law and reveal sin through the law, but rather the opposite. That is, it forces one to that which is beyond the law and to that which is impossible for the law. What is that, Dr. Luther? Is it not that which Paul often teaches to the Romans—that is, that we are released and freed from the law through the grace of Christ or through the body of Christ? Is it not the fact that we have become alive in Christ through the Spirit? . . . If [88] it pertains to the grace of Christ to have repentance in Christ's name, how can it pertain to the law? That is impossible, as Paul often teaches in Rom. 7 [:4ff.], 8 [:2–3], and elsewhere.

One sees and grasps the blindness of Dr. Luther. He is a blind leader of the people. He hears, but has not heard how to fit things together. He does not know how the harp harmonizes with the lutes. I have long thought that Dr. Luther and his followers would so mishandle the grace of Christ's name that they would say that to repent in the name of Jesus Christ means to learn what sin is from the law. And you poor fellows, do you not understand that he who repents in the name of Jesus Christ perceives through the passion of Christ the greatness and dreadfulness of his sins better and more fundamentally than he who has read, heard, or rummaged through the law for a thousand years? I ask you brethren whether it could ever be possible to understand sin rightly (namely, as sin which is wicked) without an understanding of Christ's passion, and without the knowledge which understands the wonderful grace of God and of Christ the crucified?

. . . .

Dr. [89] Luther must not understand one of these—that is, either that repentance through the law does not justify nor bear

16. See above, p. 96.

fruit to life; or that repentance through the name of Christ is a fruitful and divine repentance. For Luther combines the two sayings (to repent through the naked law, and to repent through the name of Jesus). Thus, the wiseacre gives to the law more, indeed precisely that which Moses, David, and other prophets, Christ, and the apostles take from it. Or he takes from repentance in the name of Jesus what the apostles and the disciples in Acts give to it.

Thus you should know that the name of Jesus is a name of salvation. To repent in the name of Jesus does not mean merely to call on the name of Jesus as did those of whom it is said, "Not everyone who says Lord, Lord" [Matt. 7:21]. Rather, to call on the name of Jesus or to repent therein is to know the Lord Jesus in the way Paul says: No one can say, "Jesus is Lord or Messiah" except in the Holy Spirit [I Cor. 12:3] who thus effects repentance in Jesus' name which is perceived.

. . . .

Repentance [90] is thus pointed out. And it is proved that genuine repentance does not occur through the revelation of the law, but rather in the name of Jesus and the Spirit of God. This basic point is everywhere in the prophets, evangelists, and books of the apostles. I [91] am amazed how Dr. Luther staggers! For he thinks he goes most firmly! I think he does not know what it means to be baptized in the name of Jesus. Perhaps that also gives him a reason for treating the baptism of Christ so lightheartedly that he baptizes children who do not understand their evil desires —to say nothing of their understanding the death of their evil desires through Christ![17]

. . . .

Dr. [93] Luther: These prophets "do not accept what God gives them, but rather what they themselves choose."[18]

Karlstadt: . . . Who does not know that the Lord God has certainly forbidden and taken away our self-chosen and self-selected mortification and service? For the Scripture clearly reads thus: You shall not do what seems good to you, or what you consider good (Deut. 12 [:8]; Num. 15 [:39]; Matt. 15 [:7–9]; Isa. 29 [:13]). . . . That is what I teach. That is what I preach. That is what I write. Now if I do not act accordingly, Dr. Luther should

17. See above, n. 7. Karlstadt apparently stopped baptizing infants at Orlamünde.

18. See above, p. 96.

censure me, even though he wants his work to go uncensured, when his doctrine is right.[19] I, however, hope that [94] both doctrine and work will be noticeable in me by God's grace. I say that without boasting.

. . . .

DR. LUTHER: "They wear gray cloaks."[20]

KARLSTADT: How does a common garment hurt me? With a gray cloak I do not announce any suspect holiness as Dr. Luther does with his holy cowl.

DR. LUTHER: "They use force, compulsion, and lies a great deal."[21]

KARLSTADT: I think that is wrong of Luther if he is to speak honestly. Tell me, Luther: Where have I used force here? Who has bought a gray cloak to please me? If I placed salvation in a gray cloak, I would not have mocked the monks' cowl, nor thrown away the surplice. Nevertheless, I well know that one deceives many simple people with costly clothes, and that many fools judge one's person, knowledge, and holiness on the basis of clothes. Regardless of how capable he is, he who wears cheap clothes is a fool and ass to the world. If, however, a fool wears velvet, he is considered noble and intelligent. Now if I can endure the fact that the world despises me, what concern is it of Luther's? Nevertheless, it is not so incongruous with the example of Christ and the life of the apostles to wear a gray peasant's cloak as to wear things made of scarlet, satin, silk, camels' hair, velvet, and gold. Those who preach in simple clothes do not give any offense or hindrance to the Word, nor do they bring anyone to the Word[22] through costly display (to the disgrace of the Word). For I could say this: You seek the Word of God not because it is true, but because you wear golden vestments.

Now Dr. Luther should also know that I (God be praised) have a horror of adornment which once almost seduced me [95] and brought me into sin.[23] And I thank God for that, although no garment damns me or makes me holy.

19. See n. 5.
20. See above, p. 96.
21. A summary of several charges, apparently, rather than a quotation from Luther. See above, pp. 102–6, 122.
22. That is, attract anyone to become a preacher (see below, pp. 135–36).
23. In his early academic years, Karlstadt loved ostentatious display (see *ABK*-S, p. 14).

What, however, would Dr. Luther think if I wrote that the lust for superabundant clothes damns? Or that we should not have more than one garment and one livelihood? Or that what we have beyond that is an excess and is no less sin than an excess of food? I know very well that a proud garment encourages the proud flesh. A costly style of dress is suspect and announces an inward evil in the soul.

DR. LUTHER: "They would be as peasants and carry on with similar foolish nonsense."[24]

KARLSTADT: . . . Would to God that I were a true peasant, husbandman, or craftsman so that I ate my bread in obedience to God, that is, in the sweat of my brow. But I have eaten from the toil of poor people for whom I have done absolutely nothing in exchange. Moreover, I have not had anyone at hand ready to assist them and I could not protect them. Nonetheless, I received their labor in my house. If I could, I would return to them everything that I received.

God commanded Adam to work, and that command refers to the work of the field. It seems to me that all of us are equally obligated to obtain our livelihood thereby in sorrow. And no one is excused, however high he is or may be, unless he is chosen by God for another office or is prevented by divine command. And such work is an honest mortification of the flesh commanded by God. . . .

I [96] thank God that his divine grace has graciously brought me to the frame of mind where I would gladly do [peasants'] work now without dread of what the whole world says. What do you think, Luther? Are not blisters on your hands more honorable than golden rings?

I am amazed that some people forsake work because of preaching and go about idly. I am amazed that they do not read that Christ was a carpenter and practiced carpentry, that so many prophets were naive peasant folk, and that it is prophesied that one would say, "I am a husbandman" (Zech. 13 [:5]). Was the one who preached the most the greatest of the apostles? Is it not the one who said, "We have not eaten bread without paying" (II Thess. 3 [:8])? What will our pastors say to that? Will they not

24. See above, p. 96.

say: "Indeed, we work; therefore we take money for it"? Therefore I ask whether Paul did not also do that? If he did, why did he say, "I have eaten no bread without paying, but rather with toil and labor I have worked day and night so that I would trouble no one"? How does that please you, Luther? You who dare to write, as I am informed, that a preacher may demand and take two hundred gulden per year.[25]

How does it stand with the advice you wrote? Did the prophets teach for the sake of gold? Is your advice better than the doctrine and advice of St. Paul? Or are you God's new adviser? Christ permitted the evangelists or apostles to receive food. But you go beyond Christ and permit some to take a magnificent and sumptuous table and two hundred gulden in addition. Paul says we should keep away from such disorderly bellies ([II Thess. 3:6]), but Luther encourages such disorderly grease-bellies. Paul says that one should imitate him by preaching and working, and he leads the preachers to consider the poverty of Christ. But Dr. Luther says that working is foolish nonsense and he leads the covetous bellies from Christ to the money chests. That is where their God dwells for whose pleasure or service they preach. They are silent or preach as avarice prompts them.

. . . .

Dr. [100] Luther: "However, we must see to it that we retain Christian freedom."[26]

Karlstadt: There Dr. Luther bends forward and hopes to blow me over. But he does not know that my understanding of Christian freedom is as true, good, and certain as Dr. Luther's ever was. And in order to do battle with the noisy ranter, I assert that Christian freedom consists not only in the knowledge of Christ, but also in a godly understanding of every truth of God. Paul and Christ teach that. Nevertheless, the highest freedom and genuine redemption are in the knowledge of the truth who is God's Son.

Just as freedom comes without works, so it would be disgraced and betrayed (as not being genuine) if its works did not follow.[27]

25. A considerable salary. The provost of All Saints, who had the highest income of all sixty-four clerics at All Saints, earned 200 gulden a year. Karlstadt, as archdeacon, was second with about 127 gulden per year. See *ABK*-B 2, 530.

26. See above, p. 97.

27. See n. 5 above.

Therefore Christ says: Either make a good tree and good fruit or a bad tree and evil fruit (Matt. 7 [:17–20]). For it is impossible for one to have genuine freedom in connection with a [biblical] truth and bring forth a work which is deceitful, evil, and contrary to the character of that known truth. Also, freedom cannot remain for long without its own works.

I do not make a conscience [free] through external works, but I convict the lying and false faith which boasts of freedom and yet is a prisoner of the devil whose he is and whose work he does.

The fruits of true freedom are according to the peculiar character of each [biblical] statement or truth. Common to all fruits is the fact that they truly confess the inward tree. Nevertheless, there is no confession which makes a good tree, just as little as apples or leaves make a good apple tree.

He who knows Christ has become free through the knowledge of Christ; and he walks in the works of Christ. But he does not become a Christian through works, just as one does not become a Christian through humble service, good deeds, help, or financial assistance, etc. Through the lack of such works, however, one would demonstrate that he is imprisoned in his heart to perishable [101] goods and to the devil and would attest that he has not yet become free in the truth.

When [biblical] truths are known, they make the heart free from error and from the prison of the devil and of creatures (I John 3 [:3, 8–10; cf. John 8:32])—albeit no further than one comprehends and adheres to the truth. In other things, therefore, the heart remains imprisoned. This happened to St. Peter who was called blessed and Satan in one hour (Matt. 16 [:17, 23]). . . .

There are other genuine statements of God which should be understood clearly according to the text.[28] These also make one free and unencumbered when they are known. They also have their works from the same statements. One is that concerning government—what government is, how it exists and proceeds. For judges who know God's order, in which God has established them, become free through a knowledge of the truth. They become good judges through the understanding of their office, as do bishops through a knowledge of their office. But they must both sprout up with good works, although it is not that they become judges or bishops through

28. That is, literally, not figuratively.

their works. For true understanding gives [102] birth to good works; good works, on the other hand, do not give birth to a good understanding.

But the works (as fruits of a good tree) reveal the understanding or tree, and glorify God. We judge others according to their works. Thus we say: There is a righteous prince or judge, for he does not consider the person, take bribes, or plug his ears, and he hears the complaint of the orphans and unfortunate. He helps each person obtain his rights.

However, when we do not notice such fruits in the prince or when we see the opposite (when for instance the prince takes a bribe, prefers one person to others, angrily addresses and frightens the poor, etc.) then we know that he is a false judge imprisoned by the devil. We know that he has a perverted mind.

No one hears me say that I make anyone's conscience [free or righteous] through any kind of work. For I assert that righteousness and freedom come from hearing and receiving as Christ and Moses teach.

I do, however, judge by the works. If I judge someone incorrectly, the deficiency lies in my knowledge and not in [his] works. For the truth stands: 'You will know them by their fruits" [Matt. 7:16]. If I understood the fruits correctly, then not one little hair of my judgment and verdict would be deficient.

Indeed there is more that comes from the fruits. One can examine himself and learn the state of his righteousness—that is, the righteousness of the heart which should generate works or fruits. It is true that, with reference to works, Scripture does not teach that we should serve ourselves with them, but rather that we should serve others. Nor does it teach that we become godly through them, but rather that we have an external witness of the power of our righteousness as it should demonstrate itself when it is genuine. For the free Christian stands not only before his God and before his conscience; he also stands on earth before the congregation of God.

Those who promote works, if they are believers, promote works not because freedom is born through works or because the conscience becomes righteous through works, but rather because freedom is thereby demonstrated to the glory of God and the neighbor is aroused to praise and glorify God. A sackful of Scriptures teach that. . . .

Conclusion: Karlstadt, Luther, and the Perennial Debate

Whenever dreamers attempt to alter the status quo, conflict inevitably erupts. Reactionaries regularly resist all change. Conservatives, hoping to preserve the best from the past, consent to modest or occasionally even major innovation. Liberals strive for substantial change but insist that progress be orderly, gradual, and within established structures. Radicals demand an immediate and total restructuring of the entire system.

LIBERALS AND RADICALS

The most recent version of the perennial debate between liberals and radicals surfaced in the civil rights and anti-Vietnam movements toward the end of the turbulent sixties. The debate raged at many levels. Distinguished scholars such as Richard Schaull of Princeton University and John C. Bennett of Union Theological Seminary crossed scholarly swords politely at college colloquies.[1] Black caucuses hotly debated the relative merits of a liberal versus a radical strategy. The faculty member who enjoyed good communication with his students but was unwilling to purchase explosives for the Weathermen often found himself hard

1. The papers by Schaull, Bennett, et al. are printed in John C. Raines and Thomas Dean, *Marxism and Radical Religion* (Philadelphia: Temple University Press, 1970). In his introduction, Raines noted that the most basic disagreement at the conference (held at Temple University in April 1969) was not between Marxists and Christians, but "between those of a liberal or establishmentarian persuasion and those of a radical antiestablishmentarian attitude."

pressed to show that reform was better than revolution. Churchmen publicly repented of the gross sin of liberalism.[2] Nathan Glazer of Harvard, on the other hand, stubbornly announced that recent events had *de*radicalized him—surely a counterrevolutionary admission in 1970![3] A philosopher at UCLA wrote a book advancing radical liberalism as the solution.[4] And a well-known magazine arranged a symposium to answer the question: "Liberals versus Radicals: Is There a Radical Difference?"[5]

In the last few years, the debate has subsided somewhat, but the issues remain. When a group of distinguished religious leaders met for the Aspen Interreligious Consultation on World Hunger and Global Justice in June 1974, there was sharp disagreement over the best solution to recommend. Some participants were optimistic that affluent persons and nations would reform present international economic structures. Others believed that the only meaningful solution lay in drastic restructuring produced by massive pressure from the poor of the earth.[6] The next year, Evangelicals for Social Action devoted their third national workshop to a discussion of the liberal-radical debate over strategy.[7] If, as Frederick Herzog predicted in 1976, Liberation Theology becomes highly influential in North America, this debate will undoubtedly become more explicit and intense again.[8]

Liberals and radicals clashed over the place, the pace, the personnel, and the methods for effecting change.[9] Perhaps the

2. C. Wayne Zunkel, "Reflections of a Sometime Liberal," *Brethren Life and Thought*, 14 (1969), 87–91.

3. Nathan Glazer, "On Being Deradicalized," *Commentary* (October 1970), pp. 74–80.

4. Arnold S. Kaufman, *The Radical Liberal: New Man in American Politics* (New York: Simon & Schuster, 1968). See also Paul Kurtz's editorial, "The Radical Center," *The Humanist*, 30, no. 3 (May/June 1970).

5. Paul Kurtz, "Liberals versus Radicals: Is There a Radical Difference," *The Humanist*, 30, no. 4 (July/August 1970), 7–13.

6. See *Global Justice and Development* (Washington: Overseas Development Council, 1975), p. 68.

7. For the beginnings of Evangelicals for Social Action, see Ronald J. Sider, ed., *The Chicago Declaration* (Carol Stream: Creation House, 1974).

8. Frederick Herzog, "Birth Pangs: Liberation Theology in North America," *Christian Century* (December 15, 1976), pp. 1120ff.

9. In this book, I do not use liberal in the classical sense of a person concerned with religious, political, and social freedom. For this usage, see John Plamenatz's article, "Liberalism," in the *Dictionary of the History of Ideas*, ed. Philip P. Wiener (4 vols.; New York: Scribner's, 1973), 3:36–61 (cf. esp. pp. 51–52 and the bibliography on pp. 60–61). Nor do I use radical

most significant difference between the liberal and the radical today has to do with their differing evaluations of the possibility of meaningful change *within* present societal structures.[10] Whereas the liberal sees real hope in effecting genuine, albeit gradual change within the system and consequently works for reforms, the radical despairs of changing what he regards as the almost totally corrupt status quo and therefore attempts to undermine the system and/or build alternate structures and new counter-communities.[11] Sometimes—but certainly not always—this disagreement over the possibility of changing the system results from a more fundamental divergence over ultimate goals; the more sweeping the changes desired, the less possible it may seem to effect them from within the system.

The other three points of difference can also be significant. The liberal is willing to obtain desired innovations in small incremental stages; the radical demands immediate revolution. Speaking of social and political rights, John Plamenatz notes: "The liberal is more concerned than is the radical that attempts to extend the rights should not emasculate or even destroy them while the radical is more concerned that they should be extended quickly."[12] Then too the liberal attempts to introduce change by converting or join-

---

in the way John W. Derry does in *The Radical Tradition: Tom Paine to Lloyd George* (New York: Macmillan, 1967): "Radicalism springs from the enlightenment of the eighteenth century, with its faith in human reason and the perfectibility of man" (p. ix). I use "liberal" and "radical" exclusively to connote two divergent strategies which disagree over the place, the pace, the personnel, and the role of compromise in producing change.

10. For one example of the "New Left" critique of "Corporate Liberalism," see Arthur G. Gish, *The New Left and Christian Radicalism* (Grand Rapids: Eerdmans, 1970), pp. 23–48.

11. Rosemary R. Ruether calls the radical option "apocalyptic": "Every movement that preaches the irreformability of the present system and its total corruption, that believes that the only solution is radical overthrow and reconstitution of the world on an entirely new and different basis is apocalyptic." *The Radical Kingdom* (New York: Harper & Row, 1970), pp. 9–10. The "system" however is a nebulous concept. In fact it is an almost infinite set of concentric circles. The "radical" who concludes that present political machinery is so ineffective that civil disobedience offers the only viable recourse has despaired of part of the system (i.e., of current political processes). But if he does not seek to avoid the penalty for his civil disobedience, he still accepts the society's basic legal machinery. In his *Radical Liberal*, Kaufman calls for radical restructuring of fundamental American institutions (and thus rejects basic aspects of the present system) but he believes this reconstruction can occur through the established processes of American democracy (hence he accepts a more fundamental segment of the present system).

12. Plamenatz, "Liberalism," p. 53.

ing the powerful elite; the radical hopes for change from the bottom up via the powerless, underprivileged masses. Finally, the radical despises politically expedient compromise which the liberal regretfully accepts as necessary.[13]

Can this vigorous contemporary debate between liberals and radicals shed light on the bitter disputes of earlier ages? Gordon Rupp is undoubtedly correct in warning that "to press home an historical analogy does indeed demand a knowledge, a skill, and a delicacy comparable with that of a surgeon operating on the brain."[14] Many pitfalls await any attempt to develop an analogy between sets of events separated by centuries or millennia. For one thing, the analogy may obscure as well as illuminate. One does not need to be an unqualified admirer of that murderous, thieving horde of peasants to realize that even though one may call Luther liberal or even radical because of his demand for extensive change in matters religious, he was vigorously conservative in matters sociopolitical. Imposing contemporary concepts on an earlier his-

13. "Young radicals have taught us anew the validity and perhaps the ultimate relevancy of activity outside the power structures in preference to the compromises which so often accompany inside participation." Dale W. Brown, "The Radical Reformation: Then and Now," *Mennonite Quarterly Review*, 45 (1971), 258. See too Zunkel, "Reflections of a Sometime Liberal," p. 89. The question of compromise, however, is not simple. As Paul Kurtz points out ("Liberals versus Radicals," *The Humanist*, 30, no. 4, 11), violent radicals—Marxists, for instance—compromise with means for the sake of ends.

For an analysis of different types of recent radicalism, see the following: Peter L. Berger and Richard J. Neuhaus, *Movement and Revolution* (Garden City: Anchor Books, 1970), esp. pp. 134–45. In *The Making of a Counter Culture* (Garden City: Anchor Books, 1969), pp. 56ff., Theodore Roszak distinguishes between "the mind-blown bohemianism of the beats and hippies" and the "hard-headed political activism of the student New Left." Ruether speaks of the "hippie-yippie" side of the movement and the New Left (*The Radical Kingdom*, chaps. 14, 15). Within the latter category, one must distinguish two types of political radicals: (1) those who espouse revolutionary violence (e.g., Marxists); and (2) those who are equally political and equally opposed to the present system but who express their political radicalism via the building of alternative social structures (see, for instance, Susanne Gowan, George Lakey, William Moyer, and Richard Taylor, *Moving Toward a New Society* [Philadelphia: New Society Press, 1976]). For a good example of communitarian radicals, see Calvin Redekop's excellent sketch of the Society of Brothers in "Church History and the Contrasystem: A Case Study," *Church History*, 40 (1971), 62–65. Cf. also, Stephen Goode, *Affluent Revolutionaries: A Portrait of the New Left* (New York: New Viewpoints, 1974) and Edward E. Ericson, Jr., *Radicals in the University* (Stanford: Stanford University, Hoover Institution Press, 1975).

14. Gordon Rupp, *The Old Reformation and the New* (Philadelphia: Fortress, 1967), p. 7.

torical period runs the risk of distorting the past. Certainly one should not suppose that careful study of past analogies will enable one to predict the outcome of current struggles. Finally, one risks the possibility of history becoming propaganda. One church historian recently warned that the historian may develop analogies to contemporary developments in order to win "applause for relevance and, at the same time, provide himself with a soapbox from which either to denounce or celebrate contemporary radicalism."[15]

To forget this warning would be foolhardy. On the other hand, excessive timidity may mean missing an opportunity to illuminate and increase our empathy for events of the distant past. Furthermore, the past may also provide fresh insight into the present. That there are significant analogies between the present liberal-radical quarrel and earlier debates is clear. In fact, this debate is a perennial one. To be sure, every age is unique. Hence the debate never recurs in identical language. But a cursory glance at the abolitionist movement and the French debate during the July Monarchy and the Second Republic—to select two instances at random from a vast array of possibilities[16]—reveals striking analogies both to the contemporary and the sixteenth century debate.

In his book on *Lincoln and the Radicals*, T. Harry Williams contrasts moderates such as Lincoln with the radical abolitionists:

> The moderates were typified by Lincoln. . . . They advocated the gradual extinction of slavery, compensated emancipation and colonization of the Negroes in another land. They detested slavery, and believed the institution could not survive the strain of a long civil war. But they feared and distrusted the revolutionary ardor of the radicals and the spirit of fanaticism that was inherent in the abolitionists.[17]

The abolitionists, for their part, demanded the immediate end of slavery even if it cost civil war and the destruction of the Union.

15. Ernest R. Sandeen, "John Humphrey Noyes as the New Adam," *Church History*, 40 (1971), 82.

16. One could also include the Puritan Revolution. See for instance, Michael Walzer, *The Revolution of the Saints: A Study in the Origin of Radical Politics* (Cambridge: Harvard University Press, 1965); Christopher Hill, *The World Turned Upside Down: Radical Ideas During the English Revolution* (New York: Viking, 1972).

17. T. Harry Williams, *Lincoln and the Radicals* (Madison: The University of Wisconsin Press, 1965), p. 5.

A much publicized debate (the resulting book went through several editions and influenced the entire abolitionist movement) in Cincinnati in 1845 typifies the liberal-radical struggle among American Christians concerned about slavery. On the one side was Jonathan Blanchard, a vigorous abolitionist destined to become the first president of Wheaton College. (Alma mater of Billy Graham, Wheaton College in Illinois is one of the leading evangelical colleges today.) Blanchard argued that slavery was a "social sin" which had to be abolished immediately. Church discipline should be used against slave owners or supporters of slavery. On the other side was N. L. Rice who also claimed to be an abolitionist. But he advocated gradual abolition and resettlement of slaves in Africa. Rice feared that the radical abolitionists were "upturning the very foundations of society in order to abolish slavery."[18] Knowing that Southern pastors who became abolitionists would be expelled, Rice urged that ministers not move too far ahead of their congregations.

> The debate between Blanchard and Rice was not between an abolitionist and a proslavery defender of the status quo, but between two divergent strategies for the elimination of slavery. Rice viewed Blanchard as an extremist upsetting the gradual process of amelioration of slavery effected by the preaching of the gospel, while Blanchard viewed Rice as a compromising equivocator unwilling to act on the radical implications of the gospel. To use modern terminology, it would appear that Jonathan Blanchard, the founding president of Wheaton College, was, at least on the issue of slavery, a radical rather than a liberal.[19]

Our second illustration comes from French politics during the July Monarchy and the Second Republic. Liberals advocated political rights such as the right to vote but they wanted this right restricted to "responsible" people who were well-to-do and educated. They argued that everybody would be more secure if the crucial right to vote were extended only gradually as more people acquired wealth and education and were therefore able to exercise it responsibly. Radicals on the other hand argued that the poor

18. Quoted in Donald W. Dayton, *Recovering an Evangelical Heritage* (New York: Harper & Row, 1976), p. 12.
19. Ibid., pp. 13–14.

would acquire their other rights only when they could vote. Hence they demanded this right immediately.[20]

If the liberal-radical quarrel over strategy is indeed a perennial one, one should expect that insights into and empathy for the current debate might shed light on the equally passionate sixteenth century debate over how best to implement the changes demanded by the new theological insights.[21] Using the familiar distinction between *reformatio* and *restitutio* Professor George Williams separates the magisterial from the radical reformation on the basis of what is in effect their differing evaluation of the "'establishment": "The reformers among The Old Believers and The Magisterial Reformers alike worked with the idea of *reformatio*; the Anabaptists, the Spiritualists, and the Rationalists labored under the more radical slogan of *restitutio*."[22] Believing that reform could satisfactorily alleviate the evils of the existing structures, Luther and Zwingli decided to proceed slowly and moderate their demands in order to secure the support of prince and town council. The radicals on the other hand tarried for no one in their zeal to replace existing structures and effect the restitution of primitive Christianity.[23] Revolutionary radicals like Thomas Müntzer and the leaders of the New Jerusalem at Münster in 1534–35 were willing to use force to establish an alternate society. The Anabaptists were just as insistent in their refusal to work within the medieval *corpus Christianum*, but they set about erecting alternate structures without using violence.

Nowhere was the liberal-radical debate focused more sharply

20. Plamenatz, "Liberalism," pp. 52-53.

21. For some recent attempts to suggest analogies, see the following: Paul Goodman, *The New Reformation* (New York: Random House, 1970); Walter P. Metzger, "The Crisis of Academic Authority," *Daedalus*, 99 (1970), 587–89, 602-3; Gish, *The New Left and Christian Radicalism*, chap. II (esp. pp. 52-54); Brown, "The Radical Reformation: Then and Now," 250–63; Ruether, *The Radical Kingdom*; Lowell H. Zuck, ed., *Christianity and Revolution: Radical Christian Testimonies 1520–1650* (Philadelphia: Temple University Press, 1975).

22. George Williams, *The Radical Reformation* (Philadelphia: Westminster, 1962), p. xxvi. See, however, Oliver K. Olson's objections to this analysis in his essay in *The Left Hand of God*, ed. William H. Lazareth (Philadelphia: Fortress, 1976), p. 20 and his thesis that there is a radical strain in Lutheranism: "Theology of Revolution: Magdeburg, 1550–1551" *Sixteenth Century Journal*, 3 (1972), 56–79.

23. See Franklin H. Littell, *The Anabaptist View of the Church* (Boston: Starr King Press, 1958), chap. three, "The Restitution of the True Church."

and poignantly than in the early years of the Swiss Reformation in Zurich. Conrad Grebel and other future Anabaptists were ardent supporters of the leading reformer, Ulrich Zwingli, up to the Second Zurich Disputation of 1523.[24] But when, toward the end of the disputation, Grebel pressed Zwingli to *act* on their theological consensus that the mass was not a sacrifice, Zwingli refused: "My lords [of the council] will decide the appropriate manner in which the mass is to be practiced in the future."[25] Grebel and his friends were appalled. One of them cried out: "Master Ulrich [Zwingli]! You do not have the power to reserve judgment to my lords, for judgment has already been given: The Spirit of God decides."[26] Disillusioned with their former leader, Grebel and his friends left this disputation and began to form small conventicles where they could begin implementation immediately. "For tactical reasons," on the other hand, Zwingli "preferred to gain time until the whole canton could be brought to espouse the Reform in theological depth and sociopolitical unanimity."[27]

The radicals, for their part, were moving ever closer to a total rejection of the basic medieval pattern of the state church. In 1524 they urged Zwingli to abandon the ecclesiastical structures of the past and organize promptly a new church of faithful believers. They even offered Zwingli one hundred gulden a year if he would abandon his benefice. But Zwingli preferred to "compromise with the government."[28]

Grebel's letter to Thomas Müntzer (September 4, 1524) reveals the depth of the radicals' disillusionment with Zwingli's tactical delay in implementing changes.

> The cause of all this is false forbearance. . . . [Christ] takes no heed of backsliding and anti-Christian caution, of which the most learned

24. For the text of the debate, see Donald J. Ziegler, ed., *Great Debates of the Reformation* (New York: Random House, 1969), pp. 35–69; and, for brief selections, Zuck, ed., *Christianity and Revolution*, pp. 52–54. For the massive bibliography on the rise of Anabaptism in Zurich, see Hans J. Hillerbrand, *Bibliography of Anabaptism, 1520–1630* (Elkhart: Institute of Mennonite Studies, 1962) and Hans J. Hillerbrand, *A Bibliography of Anabaptism, 1520–1630: A Sequel—1962–1974* (St. Louis: Center for Reformation Research, 1975).

25. Zuck, *Christianity and Revolution*, p. 52.

26. Ibid.

27. Williams, *Radical Reformation*, p. 90.

28. Ibid., p. 96.

> and foremost evangelical preachers have made a veritable idol and propagated it in all the world. It is much better that a few be rightly taught through the Word of God, believing and walking aright in virtues and practices, than that many falsely and deceitfully believe through adulterated doctrine.[29]

Compromising caution constitutes sinful disobedience to God's Word.

Increasingly, however, it became clear that Zwingli and the radicals disagreed over more than tactics and timing. Zwingli wanted to preserve the medieval *corpus Christianum* in a reformed Swiss commonwealth. The radicals espoused the revolutionary idea of a total separation of church and state. Centuries later the view of Grebel and his fellow radicals was to prevail. But the time was not yet. When they scorned further delay and implemented believers' baptism in early 1525, persecution, exile, and martyrdom resulted.

Activists in our day, abolitionists in the nineteenth century, English Puritans in the seventeenth century, Zurich reformers in the sixteenth century, indeed persons of every age, have struggled with their own version of the quarrel between liberals and radicals. As a short review of the events of 1521–24 will show, the debate between Luther and Karlstadt is one of the classic examples of this perennial struggle.

KARLSTADT: BETWEEN LIBERAL AND RADICAL

In the fall of 1521, more and more students, monks, and reform-minded academicians at Wittenberg decided it was time to implement some of the changes demanded by the reformers' frequent attacks on the theology and praxis of the mass.[30] The lively sermonic attack on the idea of sacrifice, the elevation of the host, and private masses by the monk Gabriel Zwilling led to an important public disputation in mid-October. Concerned for public

29. George H. Williams and Angel M. Mergal, eds., *Spiritual and Anabaptist Writers* ("Library of Christian Classics," vol. 25; Philadelphia: Westminster, 1957), pp. 74, 77. See also ibid., p. 84 where Grebel refers to "the idolatrous caution of Luther."

30. The basic documents on the Wittenberg Movement are in Nikolaus Müller, *Die Wittenberger Bewegung: 1521 und 1522* (2d ed.; Leipzig: M. Heinsius Nachfolger, 1911), hereafter cited as *WB*. For documentation for the following and for the secondary literature see *ABK-S*, pp. 153–73 and *WM*.

order and the more conservative brother, Karlstadt insisted that all the Wittenbergers must first be persuaded by preaching. To that Melanchthon retorted that there had been enough preaching; it was time to act! Turning to Karlstadt who was presiding, Melanchthon exclaimed with frustrated annoyance: "I know that your lordship also wants the thing changed." Karlstadt's reply breathes the spirit of a cautious liberal: "By all means, but without tumult and without giving opponents an opportunity for slander."[31] In order to avoid disorder Karlstadt urged that no action be taken without the consent of the Wittenberg magistracy. Change within the system would be possible if one proceeded cautiously.

But Karlstadt was overly optimistic. The elector had no intention whatsoever of meddling with the traditional liturgy at the suggestion of a few small-town professors in Wittenberg! Two months later, after the publication of more tracts, the flight of frustrated Augustinian monks and some incidental rioting, the elector still refused to sanction any innovations.

At this point Karlstadt's conservative colleagues gave him a nudge. For some time, he had asked conservative priests to take his place officiating at mass. Hoping to force him either to celebrate the traditional mass again or neglect his assigned duties, the conservatives suddenly announced that they would stop substituting for him. To their dismay Karlstadt opted for an act of civil disobedience. Ignoring an electoral prohibition against all innovation, and breaking with centuries of ecclesiastical tradition, Karlstadt celebrated the first public evangelical Eucharist in the Reformation on Christmas, 1521.

Unfortunately, historians have not always distinguished carefully enough between the acts of Karlstadt and those of the Christmas eve revelers and rioters who wished the conservative priest at All Saints pestilence and hellfire! One act in defiance of an electoral prohibition did not make Karlstadt a raving radical. He was still opposed to riot. The common charge that he forced his way into Luther's pulpit in the parish church without authorization is probably false.[32] During the first months of 1522, Karlstadt was entirely engrossed in effecting change from within the system.

31. *WB*, No. 18, p. 48.

32. "Ich auffrur hasss und flih. . . . Ich verbit auffrur" (*WB*, No. 83, p. 181). See also p. 44, n. 18; p. 10, n. *; and *ABK*-S, pp. 168–71.

Karlstadt (and other reformers such as Melanchthon) took part in extended consultations with the Wittenberg magistracy in January. The result was the important decree of about January 24 which introduced a eucharistic service modeled after Karlstadt's evangelical mass at Christmas. The common chest was also reorganized in order to provide interest-free loans to poor craftsmen and university scholarships for sons of poor persons. So elated was Karlstadt with these reforms of religious and social life that he reviewed them in his next publication (*Von abtuhung der Bylder*) and declared that God almighty had awakened the rulers' hearts and was effecting his work through them. Genuine reform from within was possible.

Part of Karlstadt's theoretical justification of these social reforms could have been written by a twentieth century liberal.[33] Although he thought that everyone was to help the poor, he emphasized the fact that it was the responsibility of the rulers in particular. He denounced those who offer charity only when the poor have almost starved. Instead, Christians must anticipate and prevent poverty by offering help before the poor are reduced to begging from door to door. Supporting a government-funded self-help program, he urged that the city provide the money to enable beggars to become established in a trade or craft. He argued on the basis of Deuteronomy 15 that these government loans need not be repaid unless the person can do so without being burdened. On the other hand, he also anticipated the modern liberal's disinclination to abolish the class structure: poor brothers are to be maintained according to their own estate! But he did call on the slave-traders at Rome and Naples to free their slaves. In short some of Karlstadt's statements apropos the poor sound progressive even today.

Unfortunately the reforms of late January represented the high point of Karlstadt's influence. Political considerations quickly frightened the elector into squelching most of the innovations Karlstadt had helped introduce. After the imperial government meeting at Nürnberg officially demanded on January 20 that he suppress the recent changes, Frederick called a meeting with the

33. For the following, see *Von Abtuhung der Bilder. . .* , ed. Hans Lietzmann, *Andreas Karlstadt: Von Abtuhung der Bilder* (No. 74; Bonn: A Marcus and E. Weber, 1911), pp. 23–27. See also Carter Lindberg, "There Should Be No Beggars among Christians: Karlstadt, Luther, and the Origins of Protestant Poor Relief," *Church History*, 46 (1977), 313–34.

Wittenberg leaders and ordered the restoration of most of the old customs. Karlstadt was forbidden to preach. At this point, Luther decided to return to Wittenberg, resume leadership of the movement, and restore order. In eight powerful sermons (selections from which are printed above in Chap. 2) in March 1522, he persuaded a majority of the Wittenbergers that delay and caution were imperative. Publicly denouncing the previous changes, he restored still more of the traditional practices—not because he preferred the old practices but because he disagreed with the timing and strategy of Karlstadt's innovations.[34] Karlstadt was livid! He wrote a fiery tract[35] denouncing the tyrants' squelching of the innovations. Although he ostensibly directed it against a Catholic by the name of Ochsenfart, everyone realized that the real target of his fury was Luther. The university establishment seized the half-printed work and forbid its publication.

At this point, Karlstadt might have apologized for his excessive zeal and worked behind the scenes as one of Luther's important lieutenants to foster as much change as possible. But he chose another route. In a move reminiscent of the turn to Eastern mysticism on the part of many of the disaffected youth from the nineteen sixties,[36] Karlstadt preoccupied himself with the German mystics. Then, after a period of intense introspection, he rejected the educational elite at Wittenberg and turned toward the comman man.[37]

Perhaps we can empathize more deeply with Karlstadt at this point if we remind ourselves of the middle-class youth who have, in the last decade, become disillusioned with the present system, dropped out of college, and joined an agrarian commune. Our sixteenth-century dropout rejected his doctoral title and adopted the role of peasant.

Karlstadt attempted to disentangle himself from the self-seeking competition and other games professors play by announcing in February 1523 that henceforth he would have no part in the granting of academic degrees. He appealed to the injunction in Matthew 23 against calling anyone master. In a book published a few weeks later, he confessed that formerly he had studied in order to write

34. See *WM*, p. 63.
35. No longer extant except for excerpts printed in *ABK*-B 2, 562–65.
36. See Roszak's chapter on "Journey to the East," *Making of a Counter Culture*, pp. 124–54.
37. For the following, see *ABK*-S, pp. 174–201.

well and win disputes. Now, however, he saw that it was wrong to study Scripture for the selfish, competitive purpose of knowing it better than another. More directly, he argued that in the universities people seek nothing but the praise of men. They become masters or doctors and give presents for the sake of worldly honor. They arrogantly refuse to sit with those who possess fewer degrees. "Although I or someone else should want to deny this, God would still . . . convince us that we bow the knee, pay money, and establish festivities and costly meals for the sake of university glory in order that we have authority with the people and are respected."[38] Contemporaries who fear that professors pursue publications and lucrative positions more ardently than truth will understand Karlstadt's attack on the academic world.

Disillusioned with the intellectual elite, Karlstadt moved to identify with the lower classes. He preferred to adopt the role of a peasant. Perhaps Karlstadt, like the contemporary long-haired radical of the sixties, realized that one must have external signs of one's rejection of established values and mores. Sometime in 1523 he put aside his academic dress, adopted the felt hat and gray garb of the peasants, and urged his neighbors to call him "Brother Andreas." In reply to Luther's satirical reference to his peasant garb, he noted that his gray cloak, unlike Luther's cowl, did not announce a suspect holiness. Furthermore, costly clothes deceive simple people who consider the cheaply dressed man a fool and the man in velvet intelligent regardless of their respective ability.

> Now if I can endure the fact that the world despises me, what concern is it of Luther's? . . . Dr. Luther should also know that I (God be praised) have a horror of adornment which once almost seduced me and brought me into sin.[39]

Like some radicals of today whose T-shirt and old jeans represent an honest revulsion from their elders' conspicuous consumption, Karlstadt was groping for a more simple life-style.

He disaffiliated himself still further from the elite and strengthened his identification with the peasantry by taking up part-time farming. "Would to God that I were a true peasant, . . . or crafts-

38. *Sich Gelassen,* eiii V, quoted in *ABK-S*, p. 177.
39. See above, p. 134.

man," he told Luther. He was aware, as are middle-class radical youth today, that the impoverished lower classes had made possible the pleasant standard of living that he had enjoyed as a member of a privileged professional class. He confessed that he had lived from the labor of impecunious peasants without giving anything in return. Farming is an "honest mortification of the flesh."

> I thank God that his divine grace has graciously brought me to the frame of mind where I would gladly do [peasants'] work now without dread of what the whole world says. What do you think, Luther? Are not blisters on your hands more honorable than golden rings?[40]

Established mores determined Karlstadt's actions less and less.

In 1523 he had opportunity to escape his financial dependence on ecclesiastical structures vigorously condemned by the reformers. Like many contemporaries who talk glibly about revolution but "ain't goin'" there, he had condemned the corrupt status quo without disentangling himself from its economic benefits. He still earned thirty-four gulden annually from endowed private masses and vigils, and he continued to hold the Orlamünde parish as a sinecure. At the invitation of the people of Orlamünde, Karlstadt moved there to be pastor in the summer of 1523.

Free at last from Luther's supervision, Karlstadt promptly proceeded to introduce his reforms without waiting for official approval and without delaying out of concern not to give offense to the weak. Images were removed from the church. He refused to baptize infants and interpreted the Eucharist as a memorial of Christ's death rather than a means of grace. He preached to his new parishioners from the Book of Acts daily and from the Gospel of John every Friday. In order that lay persons could understand and sing the Psalms, he translated them into German. Undoubtedly, he implemented the liturgical changes which he had introduced and the elector and Luther had suppressed at Wittenberg two years earlier. For a few months, in 1523 and early 1524, it seemed as if it might be possible to implement rapid change in one small area and develop a different pattern of Reformation.

In spite of their nonpolemical character, however, Karlstadt's

40. See above, p. 135.

publications of early 1524 upset Luther who complained to electoral officials. When the university demanded that Karlstadt either return to Wittenberg (which would have meant participation in condemned liturgical practices and accepting a sinecure again) or resign as archdeacon (which meant severing his last tie to established structures), Karlstadt vacillated briefly. But he quickly decided to resign and farm for a living rather than return to a compromising situation.

Unfortunately for Karlstadt, Luther and the Saxon court had come to identify Karlstadt with the far more radical Thomas Müntzer, one of the major leaders in the bloody Peasants' Revolt of 1524–25. Müntzer was already busy training his League of the Elect to destroy the status quo with violence.[41] Armed rebellion was imminent in the Saale Valley. When the elector sent Luther on a tour of the area in late August, Luther persistently refused (as the selection in Chap. 3 above indicates) to concede any difference between the spirit which destroys images and removes baptism and the spirit of Müntzer which leads to rebellion and murder.

That Karlstadt was not a violent revolutionary is indisputable. In July, Müntzer had written to both Karlstadt and the Orlamünde congregation inviting them to join the revolution. In an open letter printed at Wittenberg which *Luther had already seen before the confrontation at Jena*, the Orlamünde congregation replied that they had "nothing at all to do with worldly arms" and declared their readiness to suffer rather than fight. In his personal response Karlstadt expressed his friendship with Müntzer but categorically refused to take part in any armed alliance. He urged Müntzer to trust in God alone.[42]

Karlstadt was trapped between the radical Müntzer and the complex Luther whose conservative fear of social disorder was coming to equal his desire for religious change. Luther recommended that the princes remove Karlstadt from Orlamünde. The princes decided to go further. Ignoring Karlstadt's pleas for a public disputation, the political establishment banished Karlstadt from all of electoral Saxony. Driven out, as he complained, without trial or sentence, he vented his rage by polemicizing violently against

41. See Eric W. Gritsch, *Reformer without a Church* (Philadelphia: Fortress, 1967), pp. 91–110.

42. For this correspondence, see the note on p. 36 and p. 41, n. 9.

Luther's eucharistic doctrine and taunting him with defending the gospel with rifles.

Soon after fleeing Saxony, Karlstadt finally published *Whether One Should Proceed Slowly* (see above, Chap. 4), his belated retort to Luther's Eight Sermons of March 1522. These two statements represent a classic confrontation between a sometime-liberal whom the course of events had radicalized and a liberal who had become convinced that caution and delay were tactically expedient.[43] To Karlstadt, the liberal slogan, "Not too fast, not too soon, consider the weak" was anathema; to Luther, it represented a necessary compromise.

In the interest of brotherly love (and also the eventual success of his reformation), Luther thought it necessary to delay implementation of reforms in order not to cause offense to the weak neighbors who had not yet accepted the new ideas.[44] By patiently bearing with the weak for a time, Luther hoped to develop a broad consensus so that, as he put it, "we do not travel heavenward alone, but bring our brethren . . . with us." Pulling down images in a few small places like Wittenberg or Orlamünde does not, unfortunately, abolish them in Nürnberg and the rest of the world! Many well-meaning people, Luther believed, would eventually join the movement if one were to proceed slowly and patiently and not cause offense with precipitous haste. If one preaches first, the Word will bring about the desired changes by itself—and without uproar and tumult. Unless the hearts of all are agreed that some custom ought to be abolished, one should leave it in God's hands and wait. In short, Luther thought that the call for immediate implementation

43. But some scholars take a different view and see Luther as the radical and Karlstadt, Müntzer, and the Anabaptists as more conservative. See Carter Lindberg's "Theology and Politics: Luther the Radical and Müntzer the Reactionary," *Encounter* (Fall 1976); and Oliver Olson, in *The Left Hand of God*, pp. 10ff. Olson argues that Luther was a radical revolutionary because his doctrine of the two kingdoms theoretically undercut the religious legitimation of society. But I find the argument unconvincing. Luther accepted princes as "emergency bishops," and acquiesced in the killing of Anabaptist "heretics" (See John S. Oyer, *Lutheran Reformers against Anabaptists* [The Hague: M. Nijhoff, 1964].) The Anabaptists rejected, and Luther did not, the fundamental medieval conception of the state church.

44. For an excellent analysis of the Wittenberg discussion from 1521 on over not offending the weak, see Ulrich Bubenheimer, "Scandalum et ius divinum: Theologische und rechtstheologische Probleme der ersten reformatorischen Innovationen in Wittenberg 1521/22," *Zeitschrift der Savigny-Stiftung für Rechtsgeschichte* (1973), pp. 286 ff.

was a strategic mistake. Luther believed that the future of the Reformation depended on delay.

Karlstadt retorted that delay constituted sinful disobedience. He mocked the suggestion that one should wait to remove images and change ecclesiastical practices until a majority agreed. "I ask whether one should not stop coveting other people's goods until the others follow? May one steal until the thieves stop stealing?" Rather than have people compromise basic convictions until a consensus emerged, Karlstadt preferred a decentralized approach. Every individual and every local community should proceed on its own immediately. He hotly denied that the people of Orlamünde were obliged to delay until their "neighbors and the guzzlers at Wittenberg followed." Scorning Luther's desire to consider the effect on "Nürnberg and the rest of the world," Karlstadt announced that "each congregation, however little or great it may be, should see for itself that it acts properly and well and waits for no one." Believers must implement God's will immediately regardless of what the disobedient masses, academic theologians, or the political establishment may say.

Karlstadt considered Luther's preoccupation with not offending the weak both unbiblical and misguided. St. Paul, Karlstadt argued, did not worry about the fact that some were offended and others were sick, ignorant, and weak. Furthermore, Luther's gradualism was not even in the best interests of the weak.

> We should take such horrible things from the weak, and snatch them from their hands, and not consider whether they cry, scream, or curse because of it. The time will come when they who now curse and damn us will thank us. . . . Therefore, I ask whether, if I should see that a little innocent child holds a sharp pointed knife in his hand and wants to keep it, I would show him brotherly love if I would allow him to keep the dreadful knife as he desires with the result that he would wound or kill himself, or when I would break his will and take the knife?[45]

These words breathe the impatience of the radical.

Luther's reversal of Karlstadt's innovation of permitting the communicant to take the sacrament in his own hands offers an interesting example of the two men's differing views on the legit-

45. See above, p. 65.

imacy of tactical delay. Luther agreed with Karlstadt that touching the sacrament was not a sin. But the man who had thrown Europe into a turmoil by rejecting centuries of medieval tradition insisted that this innovation was wrong "because it caused offense everywhere." Furthermore, "the universal custom is to receive the blessed sacrament from the hands of the priest." And he demanded an end to the innovation even though it clearly symbolized his own doctrine of the priesthood of all believers, whereas the old custom he defended was more consistent with the theory of priestly mediation of grace.

This example is interesting because it shows how Luther could put his notion of not offending the weak at the service of electoral demands. Just one month earlier Frederick the Wise had instructed his representatives to demand an end to many of the innovations at Wittenberg. The elector explicitly and pointedly insisted that the sacrament not be handled by the communicant.[46] Karlstadt clearly perceived the political element in Luther's call not to offend the weak:

> Because of the weak, they say, one should delay and not proceed at all. But is that not the same as if they said that we should allow the council to determine beforehand what we should do and to what degree we should serve God?[47]

To Karlstadt, tactical delay meant serving men rather than God.

Luther's distrust of the masses and his concern for introducing change through established channels were very clear in his comment on the abolition of the mass. He approved of its abolition, but not of the "disorderly" way in which it was accomplished.

> It was done in wantonness, with no regard for proper order and with offense to your neighbor. If, beforehand, you had called upon God in earnest prayer, and had obtained the aid of the authorities, one could be certain that it had come from God.[48]

Within a month after Karlstadt's evangelical mass at Christmas, the local authorities (the Wittenberg Council) did take the appropriate legal steps to authorize the changes. For Karlstadt, who

46. *WB*, No. 92, p. 192.
47. See above, p. 64.
48. See above, p. 20.

trusted the laity and believed in local initiative far more than Luther, that was sufficient to avoid "disorder."[49] But Luther wanted electoral approval. For Karlstadt, on the other hand, any local area ruled by Christians had the obligation to make changes required by Scripture without any concern for the opinions of higher governmental authority.

My emphasis on disagreement over strategy, timing, and policy should not be taken to imply a denial of theological differences. There were some as the final three chapters of this book demonstrate. But even here, the theological differences—if one sorts out Luther's verbal overkill and clear distortion of Karlstadt's position—are not so great as has often been suggested. Furthermore, in a theological age everyone—especially theologians!—tend to conceive even essentially nontheological issues in theological terms and tend to buttress their views with biblical exegesis. Theological differences there were, but they should not be exaggerated or confused with the primary disagreement over strategy.

THE PERENNIAL DEBATE

Can we draw any general conclusions about the perennial debate between liberals and radicals?

Perhaps the most obvious, the most natural, and yet the most disturbing fact is that liberals and radicals often save their sharpest polemic and most intense dislike for each other even though they have a great deal in common. It is perfectly clear that Luther and Karlstadt were far closer in their basic theology than were Luther and his Catholic opponents. And yet the verbal attack was at least equally violent when Luther took up his pen against his former colleague as when he denounced Catholic opponents. A similar pattern has been clear in the often vituperative liberal-radical debate in our own time. One could hope that both sides might be willing to reflect more honestly on the values and goals they share.

This is difficult, of course, because both parties frequently feel that the greatest obstacles to the success of their program is the other group. Liberals often argue that it is the excesses and un-

49. See *WM*, pp. 72, 84–86 for this different attitude toward the laity and the common man.

realistic program of the radicals that frighten the majority and thus hinder implementation of the more realistic liberal policies. That Luther felt thus about Karlstadt, not to mention Müntzer, is quite clear. Conversely, radicals often feel that it is precisely the liberals' small improvements that produce the illusion of change and thereby prevent the masses from seeing the need for sweeping structural change.

There is some truth in both contentions. But it may also be true that liberals and radicals have an equally great need for each other. It is sometimes the case that a conservative majority decides to accept very significant liberal innovations because they see them as an alternative to the more revolutionary radical agenda. Furthermore, radicals play an absolutely crucial role in keeping liberals honest and judicious in the compromises they feel compelled to make. One wonders how different German history might have been if the radical Reformation which played such a significant role in English history, especially in the seventeenth century, had not been stamped out in Germany.

Radicals, on the other hand, also need liberals. One may reject Franklin D. Roosevelt's remark that a radical is a "man with both feet firmly planted in the air"[50] and still agree that radicals suffer from a lack of realism. The constant necessity of defending their strategy against the liberal charge of unrealistic idealism can strengthen the radical program. This is true even when the proper radical retort is that developing and living a new model radically different from the status quo often have in the long run a more profound effect on society as a whole than more "realistic" compromises. (One of the clearest examples is that of the courageous band of Zurich Anabaptists who defied the medieval pattern of church-state relations and developed a new model that eventually, after much abuse and persecution, became the dominant pattern of the modern world.[51]

Radicals also need liberals to keep them from what one political philosopher has called the "politics of self-indulgence." In *The Radical Liberal* Kaufman writes a blistering attack on radicals who

50. Derry, *The Radical Tradition*, p. xi.

51. See Donald F. Durnbaugh, *The Believers' Church: The History of Radical Protestantism* (New York: Macmillan, 1968); Franklin H. Littell, *The Free Church* (Boston: Starr King Press, 1957).

are more concerned with their personal purity than with the needs of the oppressed. "They are . . . too often concerned more with the state of their souls than with the preferences and welfare of those they aim to help."[52] One need only reflect on the three centuries of quietistic withdrawal and inward preoccupation that descended on the radical Anabaptists and Mennonites to realize that this is a genuine danger.

Finally Karlstadt demonstrates vividly that the liberal-radical struggle is often an internal battle waged within the individual soul. The course of events in 1522–24 radicalized Karlstadt to a significant degree. But he refused to join the Peasants' Revolt, and also declined to make common cause with the Swiss Anabaptists. He spent the last years of his life as a professor at Basle, secure within the ranks of the Magisterial Reformation in Switzerland. Thus Karlstadt lived between liberal and radical not only in the sense that he found himself trapped for a time between the cautious Luther and the radical Müntzer but also because he found himself powerfully drawn for a few years to a radical strategy which in the end he rejected.

52. Kaufman, *The Radical Liberal*, p. 51.

Selected Bibliography

Barge, Hermann. *Andreas Bodenstein von Karlstadt.* 2 vols. Leipzig: Friedrich Brandstetter, 1905.

Bubenheimer, Ulrich. *Consonantia theologiae et iurisprudentiae: Andreas Bodenstein von Karlstadt als Theologe und Jurist Zwischen Scholastik und Reformation.* Tübingen: Mohr, 1977.

Edwards, Jr., Mark U. *Luther and the False Brethren.* Stanford: Stanford University Press, 1975.

Fife, Robert H. *The Revolt of Martin Luther.* New York: Columbia University Press, 1957.

Kriechbaum, Friedel. *Grundzüge der Theologie Karlstadts: Eine systematische Studie zur Erhellung der Theologie Andreas von Karlstadts (eigentlich Andreas Bodenstein 1480–1541), aus seinen eignen Schriften entwickelt.* ("Theologische Forschung," No. 43.) Hamburg-Bergstedt: Herbert Reich Evangelischer Verlag, 1967.

Müller, Karl. *Luther und Karlstadt: Stücke aus ihrem gegenseitigen Verhältnis.* Tübingen: J. C. B. Mohr, 1907.

Preus, James S., *Carlstadt's* Ordinaciones *and Luther's Liberty: A Study of the Wittenberg Movement, 1521–1522.* Cambridge: Harvard University Press, 1974.

Rupp, Gordon. *Patterns of Reformation.* Philadelphia: Fortress Press, 1969. Pp. 49–153.

Sider, Ronald J. *Andreas Bodenstein von Karlstadt: The Development of His Thought, 1517–1525.* ("Studies in Medieval and Reformation Thought," No. 11.) Leiden: E. J. Brill, 1974.

Index